Sweet Land of Liberty
The Spirit of Growing America

Heritage Studies 3

WORKTEXT

FOR USE WITH HERITAGE STUDIES 3 SECOND EDITION

BJU PRESS

Greenville, South Carolina

HERITAGE STUDIES 3 Worktext
For use with HERITAGE STUDIES 3 Second Edition

Coordinating Authors
Gina P. Bradstreet
Christine W. Kuhr
Debra White

Contributing Authors
Eileen M. Berry
Peggy Davenport
Stephanie J. Ralston
Dawn L. Watkins

Consultants
Marnie Batterman
Sharon V. Fisher

Project Editor
Elizabeth Bang Berg

Project Manager
Elena Emelyanova

Bible Integration
Bryan Smith
William L. Gray

Designer
David Siglin

Cover Designer
Aaron Dickey

Compositor
Bonnijean Marley

Illustrators
Caroline George
Preston Gravely
Jim Hargis
Nathan Kirsop
Kathy Pflug
Dave Schuppert
Megan Strand
Danielle Vasso

Photo Acquisition
Sarah C. Strawhorn

Photo credits appear on page 137.

© 2006 BJU Press
Greenville, South Carolina 29614

Printed in the United States of America
All rights reserved

ISBN 978-1-59166-506-9

15 14 13 12 11 10 9 8 7 6 5 4 3 2

CONGRATULATIONS

Your search for the very best educational materials available has been completely successful! You have a textbook that is the culmination of decades of research, experience, prayer, and creative energy.

The foundation

Nothing to conflict with Truth and everything to support it. Truth is the pathway as well as the destination.

The facts

Nothing overlooked. Revised and updated. Facts are used as a springboard to stimulate thoughtful questions and guide students to broader applications.

The fun

Nothing boring about this textbook! Student (and teacher) might even forget it's a textbook! Brimming with interesting extras and sparkling with color!

Contents

Government

World History

Geography

American History

Culture

Economics

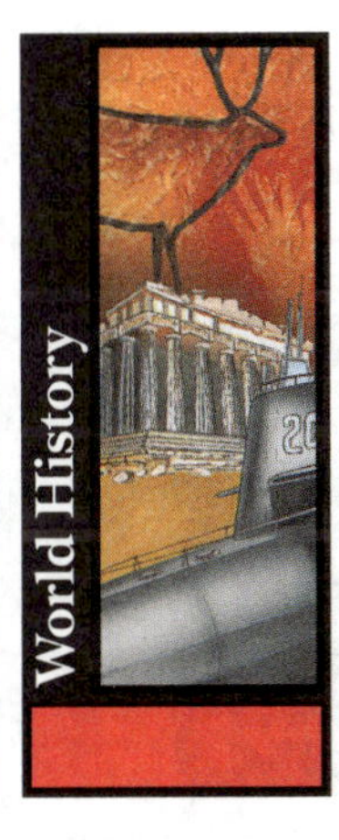

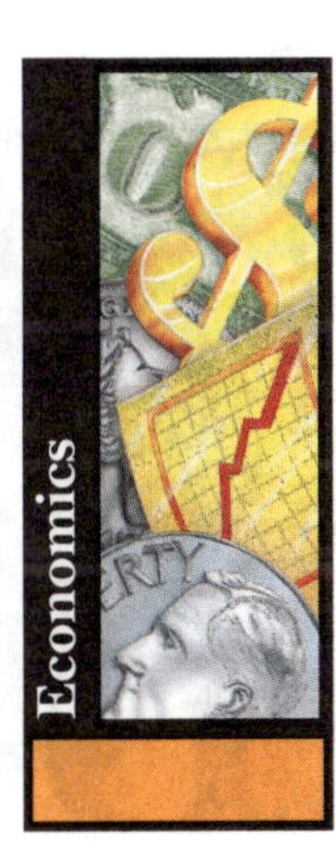

Do You Remember?

Do you remember these facts from Heritage Studies 1 and 2?

Mayflower

Columbus lands in America.

1. Christopher Columbus found a "new world" we call __A__.

2. Pilgrims seeking religious freedom sailed on the __M__.

3. Many colonists came from __E__.

4. King George taxed the colonists and sent his soldiers, called __R__.

Redcoats

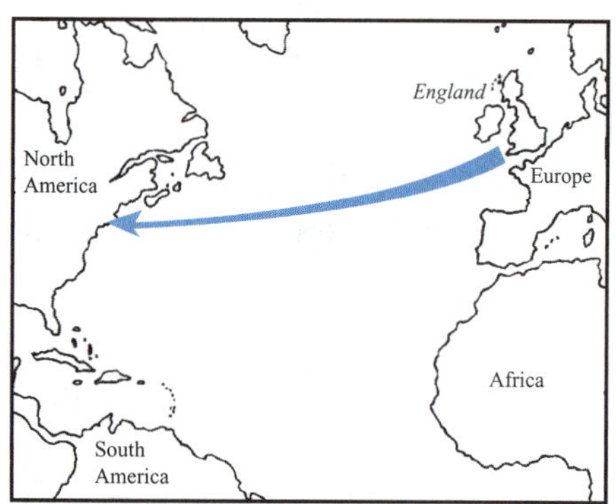
The colonists' journey

5. Colonists wanted freedom, so they met here and wrote the Declaration of __I__.

6. Laws for the new country were written in the __C__.

Constitution

7. George Washington was the first president of the United States of __A__.

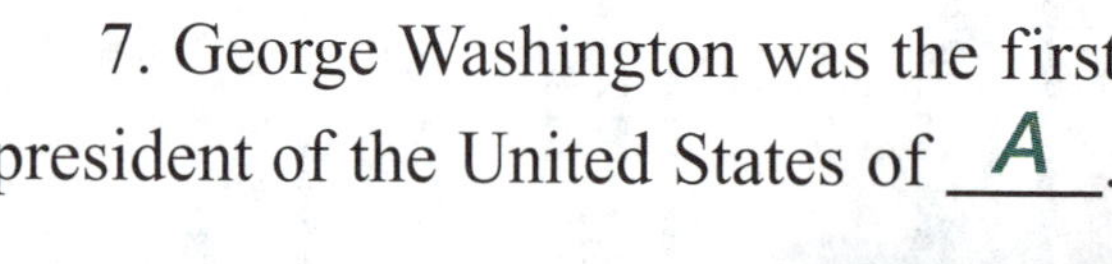

Independence Hall

President George Washingtion

Mount Vernon

Study the floor plan of Mount Vernon. Answer the questions using the key.

1. How many fireplaces does the house have? ________________

2. On which floor is there a chimney without a fireplace? ________________

3. How many pillars hold up the roof of the piazza? ________________

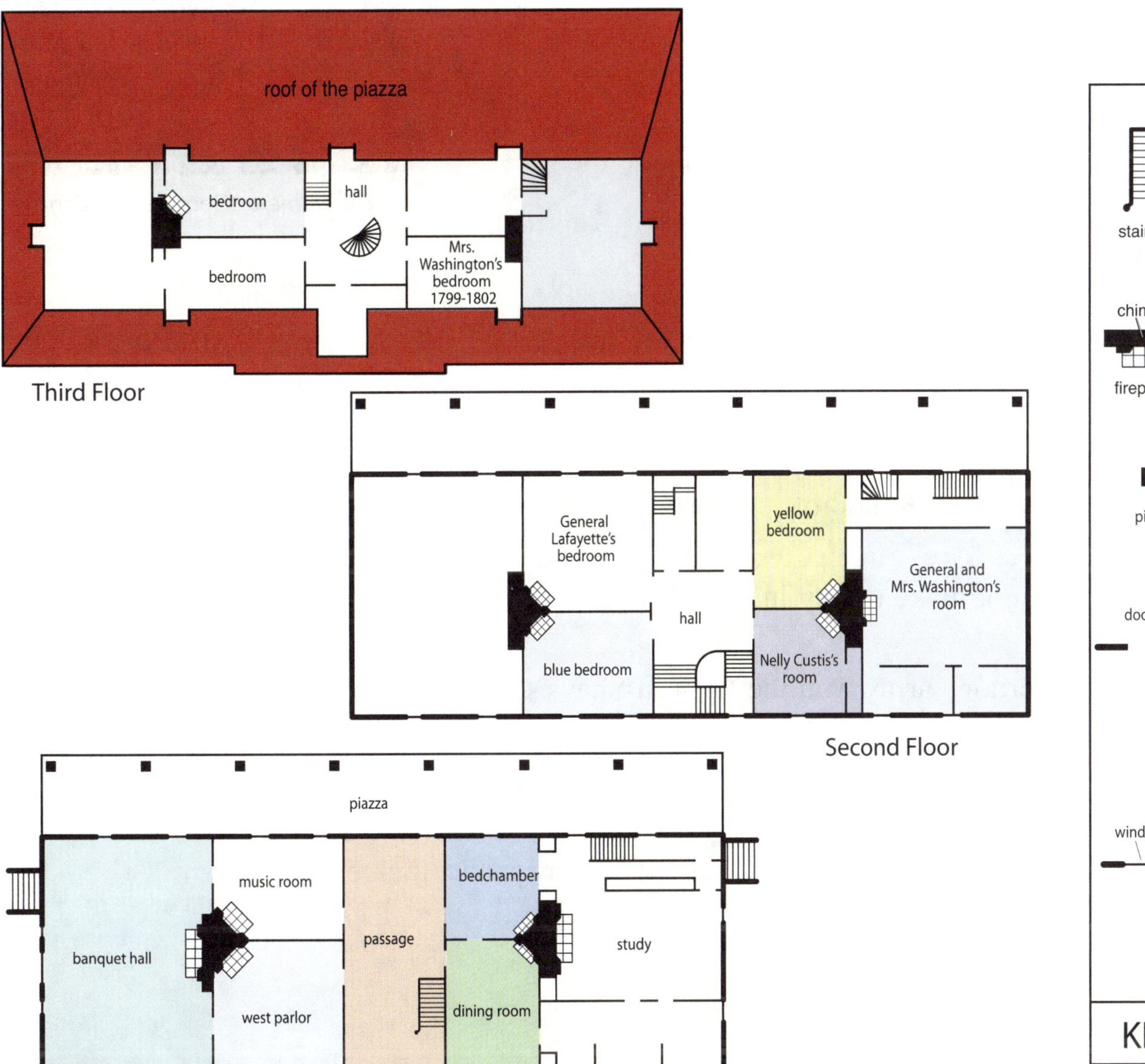

Mount Vernon: The home of George Washington

New Country

Fill in the blanks using the word banks (text pages 2–5).

bells   money   silver   taxes

1. The leaders in Massachusetts made the

   people pay in ________________.

2. The leaders of the thirteen states needed to

   get ________________.

3. The leaders in the thirteen states made the

   people pay ________________.

4. When America defeated the redcoats, the ________________ of Philadelphia
   rang.

The home of George Washington

government   Rebellion   Shays   Vernon

5. "You cannot make us pay in silver!" said Daniel ________________.

6. The governor's army won the fight in Shays's ________________.

7. George Washington wanted to stay home at Mount ________________.

8. George Washington had to go help his country start the new

   ________________.

The Constitutional Convention

Fill in the blanks using the word bank (text pages 6–8).

| Articles | Constitutional | Mayflower | Philadelphia | rules | Washington |

1. The old laws that kept the colonies together were called the _______________ of Confederation.

2. Men came from twelve states to the city of _______________ to write laws.

3. The meeting to make new laws was called the _______________ Convention.

4. Everyone agreed that George _______________ should be in charge of the meeting.

5. Three men made a list of _______________ for holding meetings.

6. Over a hundred years earlier, the Separatists in the New World had made rules called the _______________ Compact.

Philadelphia

Men came from twelve states to Philadelphia.

Name______________________

George Washington loved his family and his country. He chose to leave his family and his home, Mount Vernon, to serve his country at the Constitutional Convention. George Washington thought of others. He was unselfish.

Write the letter of the answer in the blank. Text pages are given with each question.

1. The leaders of the states needed money to run the country. What did they make the people pay? (3)
   A. bills
   B. farm goods
   C. taxes

2. Who started a fight because he did not want to pay taxes in silver? (4)
   A. George Washington
   B. Daniel Shays
   C. Benjamin Franklin

3. Who left Mount Vernon and went to the Constitutional Convention in Philadelphia? (5)
   A. Benjamin Franklin
   B. Daniel Shays
   C. George Washington

4. George Washington thought of others first. What word describes him? (Think About It)
   A. unselfish
   B. selfish
   C. cowardly

5. What were the rules to keep the colonies together called? (6)
   A. Articles of Confederation
   B. Mayflower Compact
   C. Independence Hall

6. What did the men at the Constitutional Convention do? (7)
   A. always agreed with each other
   B. had a party
   C. followed rules concerning the meeting

7. What were the rules made by the Separatists in the New World called? (8)
   A. Articles of Confederation
   B. Mayflower Compact
   C. Independence Hall

America the Beautiful

Katherine Lee Bates

Samuel A. Ward

Branches of Government

Name_______________________________

Fill in the blanks using the word banks (text pages 9–12).

| branches | followed | laws | Madison | obey |

1. "The Articles will not work anymore. We must write a whole new set of laws. We must write a Constitution," said James _______________________.

2. The men decided on three _______________________, or parts, of the new government.

3. One branch would make _______________________.

4. One branch would see that _______________________ laws are _______________________.

5. One branch would deal with those who do not _______________________ the laws.

The three branches of American government

| House | Senate | two | votes |

6. The branch that makes the laws was divided into _______________________ groups.

7. One group is called the _______________________ of Representatives.

8. The second group is called the _______________________.

9. The big states and the small states could not agree on how many _______________________ each state would get.

The Great Compromise

Name_______________________________

Complete the crossword puzzle using the word banks (text pages 13–15).

census   compromise   Declaration   House   yes

Across

5. An agreement that is good enough for both sides to like is a ____.

7. An important paper in American history is the ____ of Independence.

8. States have different numbers of votes in the ____ of Representatives.

9. Five states voted ____ on the Great Compromise.

10. Counting people is called taking a ____.

Articles   Convention   no   Senate   Sherman

Down

1. The author of the Great Compromise was Roger ____.

2. The meetings to write the Constitution were called the Constitutional ____.

3. Four states voted ____ on the Great Compromise.

4. Roger Sherman signed the ____ of Confederation.

6. All states have the same number of votes in the ____.

Roger Sherman

Fill in the blanks using the word banks. Text pages are given with each question.

branches   Constitution   laws   Senate   votes

1. James Madison said the Articles of Confederation would not work anymore. "We must write a whole new set of laws. We must write a ________________." (9)

2. The new government had three parts, or ________________. (11)

3. The new government would make laws, see that laws are followed, and deal with those who do not obey the ________________. (11)

4. The two groups of the government branch that make new laws are the House of Representatives and the ________________. (11)

5. In the Senate each state has an equal number of ________________. (13)

census   Constitution   Convention   Great   number

6. In the House of Representatives, votes are given according to the ________________ of people in the state. (13)

7. The ________________ Compromise decided how many votes each state would receive. (14)

8. When the government counts the people, it takes a ________________. (14)

9. The laws for the new country were called the ________________. (14)

10. The Constitutional ________________ met to write the laws for the new country. (14)

The words we speak should be kind and gracious.

(Bible principle from Ecclesiastes 10:12)

Preamble

1. Read the *Learning How* steps on text page 19.

2. See page 10 for diagram. Cut the Preamble strip on the dark lines. Fold on the dotted line. Slide the strip into the viewer on Worktext page 11.

We the People of the United States, in order to . . .	
form a more perfect union,	build the best nation possible,
establish justice,	set up fair treatment under the law,
insure domestic tranquility,	keep peace for our homes and our country,
provide for the common defense,	be ready to protect our people from attack,
promote the general welfare,	encourage well-being for everyone,
and secure the blessings of liberty to ourselves and our posterity,	and guard liberty for ourselves and others,
. . . do ordain and establish this Constitution for the United States of America.	

fold

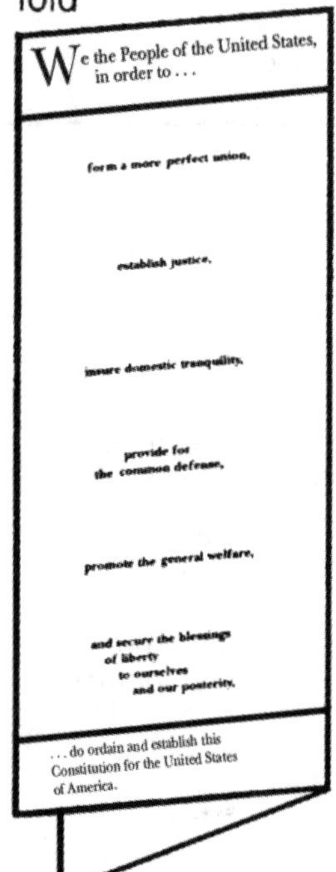
We the People of the United States, in order to . . .
form a more perfect union,
establish justice,
insure domestic tranquility,
provide for
the common defense,
promote the general welfare,
and secure the blessings
of liberty
to ourselves
and our posterity,
. . . do ordain and establish this Constitution for the United States of America.

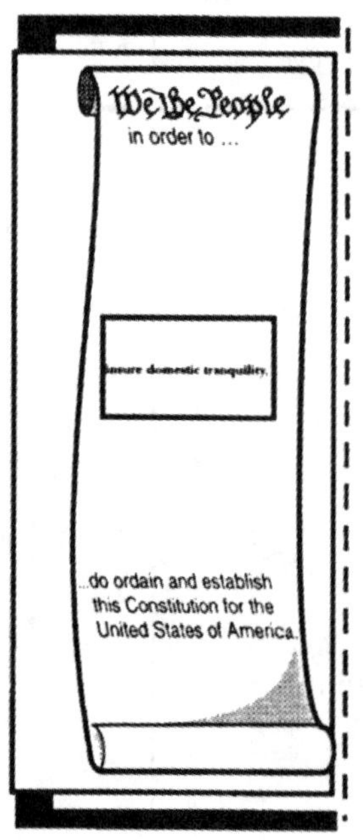
We the People
in order to . . .
insure domestic tranquility.
...do ordain and establish
this Constitution for the
United States of America.

nation
keep peace for our
homes and our country,

Preamble Viewer

Name_____________________

1. Use the viewer with the Preamble strip on Worktext page 9.

2. Cut the viewer on the dark lines. Cut out the inside boxes. Fold the viewer on the dotted line. Slide the Preamble strip into the viewer.

3. Use the viewer to memorize the sections of the Preamble. Study the meaning on the back.

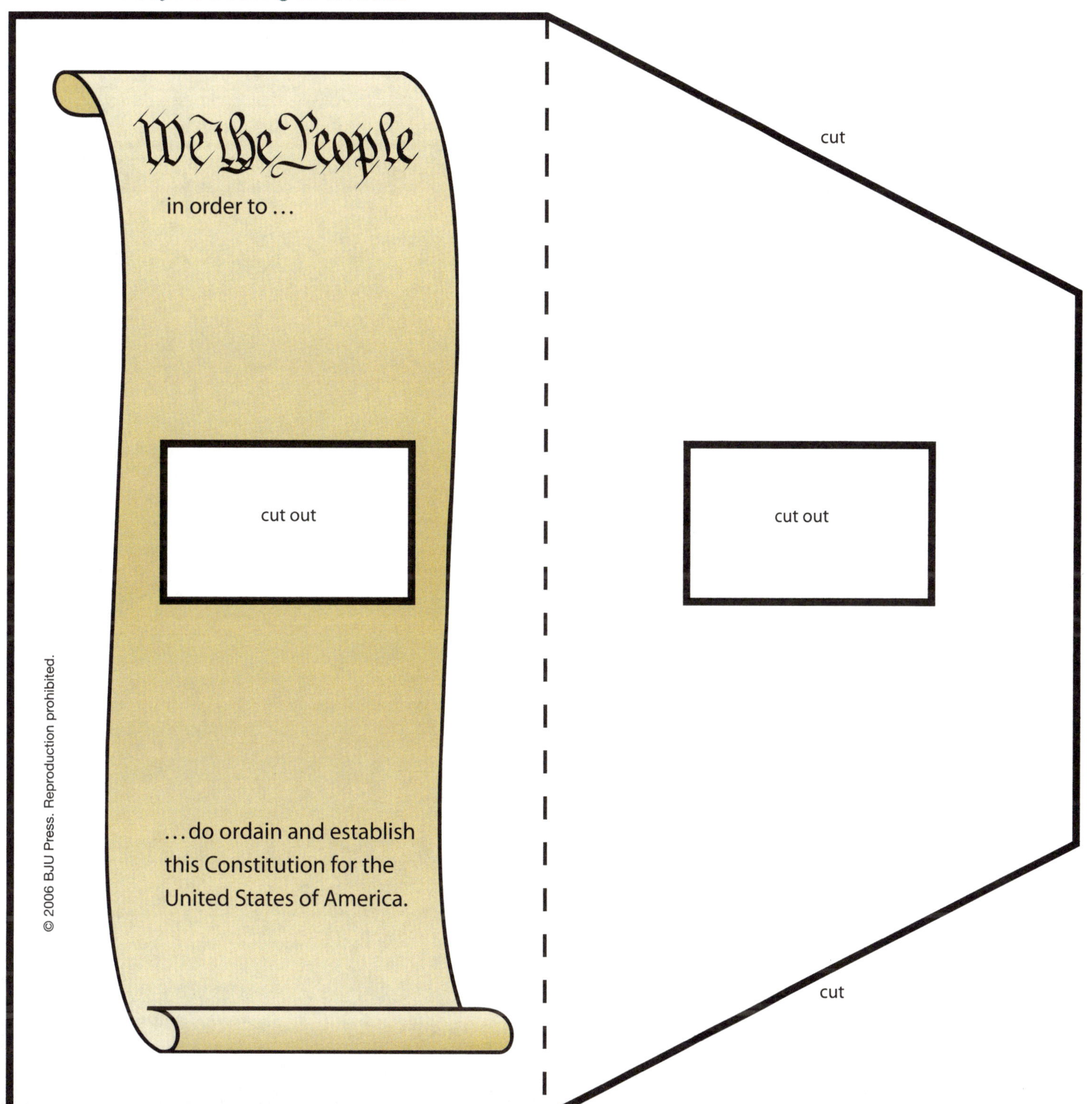

Name________________________

1. Read the Bill of Rights summary on text page 273.

2. Draw a picture telling about the one freedom in the Bill of Rights for which you are most thankful.

The Bill of Rights

Name________________________________

Fill in the blanks using the word banks (text pages 20–22).

| newspapers   nine   ratify   Washington |

1. The words of the Constitution were printed in
   ____

   _______________________________ .

2. The word that means "to approve of or agree to" is
   ____

   _______________________________ .

3. For the Constitution to become law, _______________________ states had to ratify it.

4. The first president was George _______________________ .

| freedoms   law   Madison   Washington |

5. The Constitution became "the _______________________ of the land."

6. "I will protect the Constitution," said George
   ____

   _______________________________ .

7. The Bill of Rights is a list of
   ____

   _______________________________ added

   to the Constitution.

8. James _______________________ is called the Father of the Constitution.

George Washington

James Madison

Name_______________________________

Complete the Chapter Review. Text pages are given with each question.
A. Write the letter of the answer in the blank.

_______ 1. Who said, "The Articles will not work anymore. We must write a whole new set of laws. We must write a Constitution"? (9)

A. James Madison

B. George Washington

C. George Mason

_______ 2. Who said, "Slavery brings the judgment of heaven on a country"? (16)

A. George Washington

B. George Mason

C. Daniel Shays

_______ 3. Who said, "You cannot make us pay in silver"? (4)

A. James Madison

B. George Mason

C. Daniel Shays

_______ 4. Who said, "I will protect the Constitution"? (22)

A. George Mason

B. George Washington

C. James Madison

B. Fill in the blanks using the word bank.

| census | compromise | preamble | ratify |

____________________ 5. a counting of the people (14)

____________________ 6. an agreement good enough for both sides to like (13)

____________________ 7. words that go before (18)

____________________ 8. to approve of or agree to (21)

Name__________________________________

C. Fill in the blanks using the word bank.

| branches | Compromise | Confederation | Constitution | Rights |

9. The rules to keep the colonies together were called the Articles of

______________________. (6)

10. The "law of the land" is called the ______________________. (21)

11. The new government had three ______________________, or parts. (11)

12. The Great ______________________ gave each state two votes in the Senate. But in the House of Representatives, votes are given according to the number of people in the state. (13–14)

13. The list of freedoms added to the Constitution is called the Bill of

______________________. (21)

D. Write two freedoms that are guaranteed in the Bill of Rights. (22, 273)

14. ______________________

15. ______________________

E. Fill in the circle.

16. Who was unselfish? (5)

   ○ Daniel Shays   ○ George Washington

17. How should the men of the Constitutional Convention have behaved? (7)

   ○ The men should have followed the rules.

   ○ The men should have shouted and argued.

18. What was the list of rules the Separatists wrote in the New World? (8)

   ○ the Republic   ○ the Mayflower Compact

Pay Taxes or Buy Bread?

Name_______________________

A. Lightly color the loaf of bread brown if the statement is true (text pages 24–29).

1. Paris is the capital of France.

2. Peasant farmers cried out for bread.

3. Marie Antoinette was queen of France.

4. The king and queen lived in luxury with fancy things.

5. The Bastille was a store in France.

6. Lincoln was president when Louis XVI ruled France.

B. Lightly color the loaf of bread brown if these people paid taxes.

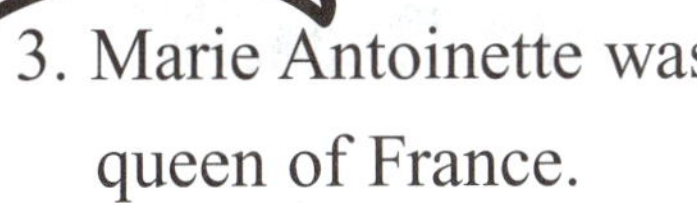

7. shopkeepers or townspeople

8. church leaders

9. peasants or poor farmers

10. Louis XVI and Marie Antoinette

11. working people

12. rich people

Name_______________________

Fill in the blanks using the word banks. Text pages are given with each question.

church   jail   luxury   Paris

1. The Bastille was a _________________. (26)

2. The capital of France is _________________. (24)

3. The French government included common people, rich people, and _________________ leaders. (28)

4. King Louis XVI and Queen Marie Antoinette lived in _________________ _________________. (25–26)

common   mob   rich   unhappy

5. The common people were _________________ with Louis XVI and Marie Antoinette. (25)

6. The _________________ of peasants killed the governor of the Bastille. (32)

7. The church leaders and the _________________ _________________ people did not pay taxes. (28)

8. The _________________ people thought that the king should not have so much power. (28)

Anonymous, 18th century. Storming of the Bastille, July 14th, 1789: Arrest of the Governor Monsieur de Launay

The queen did not want the king to listen to the common people.

The king taxed the poor people so much that they had no money left to buy bread.

Declaration of Independence

Name_______________________

A. Read this section from the Declaration of Independence.

We hold these truths to be self-evident, that all men are created equal, that they are endowed by their Creator with certain unalienable Rights, that among these are Life, Liberty, and the pursuit of Happiness.

Self-evident refers to a truth that does not need any proof or explanation. **Endowed** means "to be provided." **Unalienable rights** are rights that are not to be taken away.

B. Use this section of the Declaration of Independence and the Think About It to fill in the circle.

1. What does *self-evident* mean?
   - ○ a truth that does not need to be explained
   - ○ a term that needs an explanation

2. It is self-evident that most third graders _____.
   - ○ study history
   - ○ play the tuba

3. Which statement means it is "self-evident, that all men are created equal"?
   - ○ One must prove that all men are equal.
   - ○ No one needs to prove that all men are created equal.

4. Since all men are created equal, everyone _____.
   - ○ wears a size 8 shoe
   - ○ has the same rights

5. Who endowed or provided rights for all men?
   - ○ the president
   - ○ the Creator, God

6. What are the *three unalienable rights* guaranteed to each citizen of the United States? Fill in three circles.
   - ○ holiness
   - ○ liberty
   - ○ life
   - ○ the pursuit of happiness

The Terror

The **French Revolution** was a rebellion by the common people against the king, church leaders, and rich men. During the year of *the Terror*, even the common people were afraid of the leaders of the French Revolution, or **revolutionists**.

A. Fill in two circles to complete each statement (text pages 30 and 34).

1. The Marquis de Lafayette _____.
   - ○ was a French nobleman who fought in the American War for Independence
   - ○ brought ideas of freedom and government from America to France
   - ○ said, "Don't listen to the people"

2. The *Declaration of the Rights of Man and of the Citizen* _____.
   - ○ said that everyone should have the same rights
   - ○ said that the king and queen should have all the power
   - ○ was similar to the American Declaration of Independence

B. Fill in one circle to complete each statement (text pages 34–37 and the Think About It).

3. The French common people called their new government _____.
   - ○ the War for Independence   ○ the National Assembly

4. The National Assembly asked King Louis XVI to give up some _____.
   - ○ power   ○ of the palace

5. The year called *the Terror* was a time when common people and rich people alike _____.
   - ○ were arrested for speaking out against the French Revolution
   - ○ were safe from the revolutionists

6. Because they did not support the revolution, Louis XVI and Marie Antoinette were_____.
   - ○ sent to another country
   - ○ beheaded

7. When King Louis XVI was put on trial, _____.
   - ○ he joined the French Revolution
   - ○ he was found guilty of being against the French Revolution

The king and queen lived in the beautiful Versailles palace.

National Songs

Name_________________________

A. Use the word bank to complete this patriotic song. Sing it to the tune of "Row, Row, Row Your Boat."

blue   flag   honor   love

See, see, see, your ________________ ,

Red and white and ________________ .

Honor America, ________________ America,

Land we ________________ so true.

B. Write some words that show national pride, respect for the flag, and love for country.

freedom   Liberty Bell   brave soldiers

C. Write your own patriotic song if you wish.

Name_______________________

Match the question with the term by writing the letter in the blank. Text pages are given with each question.

A. Louis XVI   B. the Marquis de Lafayette   C. Marie Antoinette

_______ 1. Who brought ideas of freedom and government from America to France? (30)

_______ 2. Who was queen of France when the French Revolution began? (35)

_______ 3. What king was against the revolution and was beheaded? (36)

D. National Assembly   E. French Revolution   F. revolutionists

_______ 4. What was the war in France between the common people and the rich people? (37)

_______ 5. Who formed armies and fought for their rights? (38)

_______ 6. What did the French common people call their government? (34)

G. national anthem   H. *the Terror*
I. the *Declaration of the Rights of Man and of the Citizen*

_______ 7. What was the time called when the common people could not disagree with the revolution? (37)

_______ 8. What is a country's song called? (39)

_______ 9. Which paper told what the new French government believed? (34)

> *"Better is a poor and a wise child than an old and foolish king."*
> **Ecclesiastes 4:13**

Revolutionists formed armies and fought for the rights of the people.

Heritage Studies 3
Worktext—Chapter 2

America or France?

Write an *X* in the America column if the statement is true for America. Write an *X* in the France column if it is true for France. Some statements may have an *X* in both columns (text pages 41–42).

	America	France
1. This was a new nation.		
2. The people valued their freedoms.		
3. George Washington was the leader.		
4. The soldiers fought and won many battles.		
5. The people considered Napoleon Bonaparte their hero.		
6. The country was not part of the French Revolution.		
7. This was a strong, old country.		
8. Napoleon crowned or made himself ruler.		
9. People had to obey Napoleon's hard rules.		
10. Some people wished they still had a king.		

The American people elected George Washington president.

Napoleon Bonaparte made himself ruler of France.

Name_______________________________

Complete the Chapter Review. Text pages are given with each question.
A. Match the term with the description by writing the letter in the blank.

________ 1. a jail (26, 31–32)

________ 2. the capital of France (24)

________ 3. could not risk new freedom to help France (41)

________ 4. queen of France (26)

________ 5. did not help in the French Revolution (41)

________ 6. crowned himself ruler or emperor of France (42)

A. United States
B. Paris
C. Bastille

D. George Washington
E. Napoleon Bonaparte
F. Marie Antoinette

B. Fill in the blanks using the word banks.

common   disagree   rights   unhappy

7. The three parts of the French government were the _______________ people, the rich people, and the church leaders. (28)

8. The common people were _______________ that they had nothing to eat when the king and queen lived in luxury. (25–26)

9. No one was safe to _______________ with the revolution. (37)

10. Every Frenchman should have the same _______________, according to the *Declaration of the Rights of Man and of the Citizen*. (34)

governor   Lafayette   Louis XVI   Napoleon

11. _______________ was beheaded since he did not support the revolution. (36)

12. The general who made hard rules for the people was _______________. (42)

13. _______________ brought ideas of freedom and government to France. (30)

14. Peasants killed the _______________ of the Bastille. (32)

Physical Map

Name_________________________

The map key on page 285 uses different colors to show how high land is above the ocean or sea level. The dark brown means the land is high above the level of the ocean—such as a mountain. Green means the land is lower, closer to the level of the ocean—mostly flat land.

A. Fill in the circle (text pages 44–47 and 284–85).

1. Big areas of land are called _____. ○ continents ○ features

2. The earth has four _____. ○ continents ○ oceans

3. Physical features on a map were _____. ○ made by God ○ made by man

B. Put a check mark next to physical features found on the physical map on pages 284–85.

☐ roads ☐ lakes

☐ mountains ☐ rivers

C. Put a check mark next to three colors found on the physical map on pages 284–85.

☐ blue ☐ brown ☐ green ☐ purple

D. Read and follow the *Learning How* steps on text page 47. Put a check mark next to each feature found in your state. Use the map on pages 284–85.

My state is _______________________________.

- The color(s) found in my state is (are) _____.

  ☐ blue ☐ brown ☐ green

- The land in my state is mostly _____. ☐ high ☐ low

- The physical features found in my state are _____.

  ☐ rivers

  ☐ lakes

  ☐ mountains

  ☐ flat land

"The sea is his, and he made it: and his hands formed the dry land."
Psalm 95:5

Areas of America

A. Color the map using the map key. Draw the animal horn pictures from the map key onto the correct area of the map.

Map Key

● Great Forest  White-Tailed Deer

● Prairie Bison

● Rocky Mountains Bighorn Sheep

The land between the Atlantic Ocean and the Mississippi River was a huge forest. The land was thick with trees and wild animals. The area was called the Great Forest because of the great number of trees.

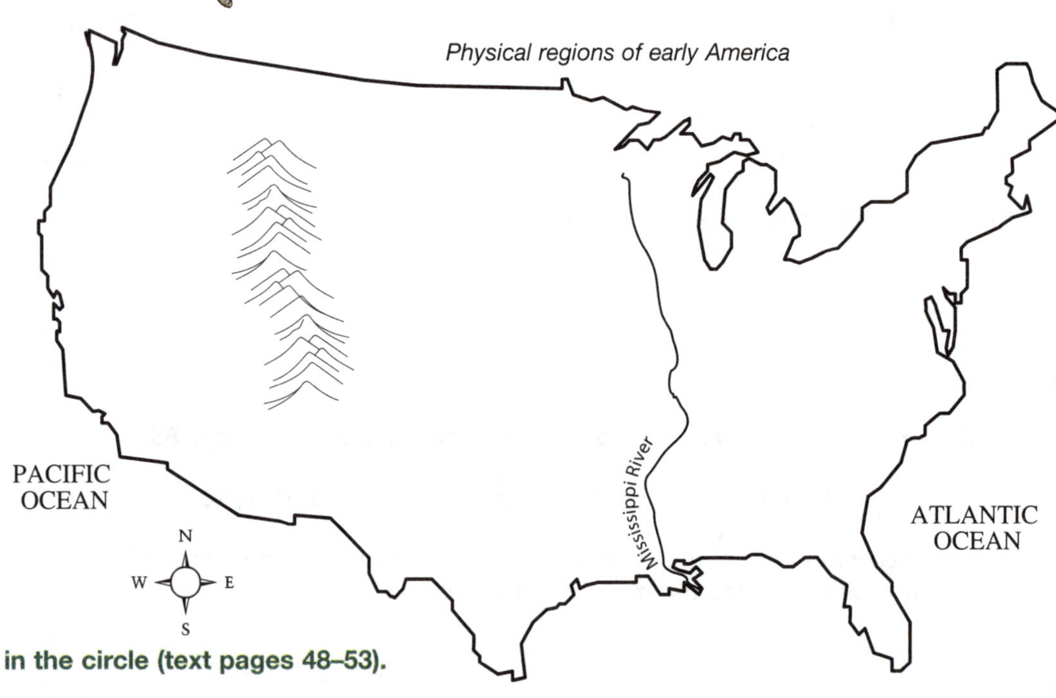

B. Fill in the circle (text pages 48–53).

1. In early America, what was between the Atlantic Ocean and the Mississippi River?

   ○ forest   ○ prairie   ○ mountains

2. What animal can be found in the forest?

   ○ bison   ○ white-tailed deer   ○ bighorn sheep

3. What is the flatter land beyond the Mississippi River called?

   ○ Great Forest   ○ Prairie

4. What animal can be found on the Prairie?

   ○ bighorn sheep   ○ bison

5. What is a place that gets only a little bit of rain each year called?

   ○ forest   ○ desert

Study Questions

A. Write the letter of the answer in the blank. Text pages are given with most questions.

____ 1. A map that shows features such as mountains and rivers is called ____. (46)
A. a road map
B. a physical map
C. a country map

____ 2. The land between the Atlantic Ocean and the Mississippi River was called ____.
A. the Great Forest
B. the Prairie
C. the Rocky Mountains

____ 3. The flat grassland with few trees beyond the Mississippi River was called ____. (50)
A. the Great Forest
B. the Prairie
C. the Rocky Mountains

____ 4. An animal that lives high in the Rocky Mountains is ____. (52)
A. a bison
B. a white-tailed deer
C. a bighorn sheep

____ 5. An animal found in the Great Forest was ____. (48)
A. a bison
B. a white-tailed deer
C. a bighorn sheep

____ 6. Two types of animals found on the Prairie were ____. (50)
A. prairie dogs and herds of bison
B. prairie dogs and bighorn sheep
C. bison and bighorn sheep

B. Write *T* if the statement is true and *F* if it is false. Make each false statement true by correcting the underlined word(s). Write the correct answer in the blank.

______ 7. It is too cold for many plants to grow in <u>the Rocky Mountains</u>. (52) ____

______ 8. There are <u>three</u> large bodies of water called oceans. (45) ____

______ 9. Big areas of land are called <u>oceans</u>. (45) ____

______ 10. God planned for <u>desert</u> animals to get water from plants. (53) ____

Bar Graph

Pioneers traveled on foot, by horse, and by train. The bar graph shows the days it took for pioneers to travel from Pioneer Bluff to Frontier Point.

Travel Time from Pioneer Bluff to Frontier Point

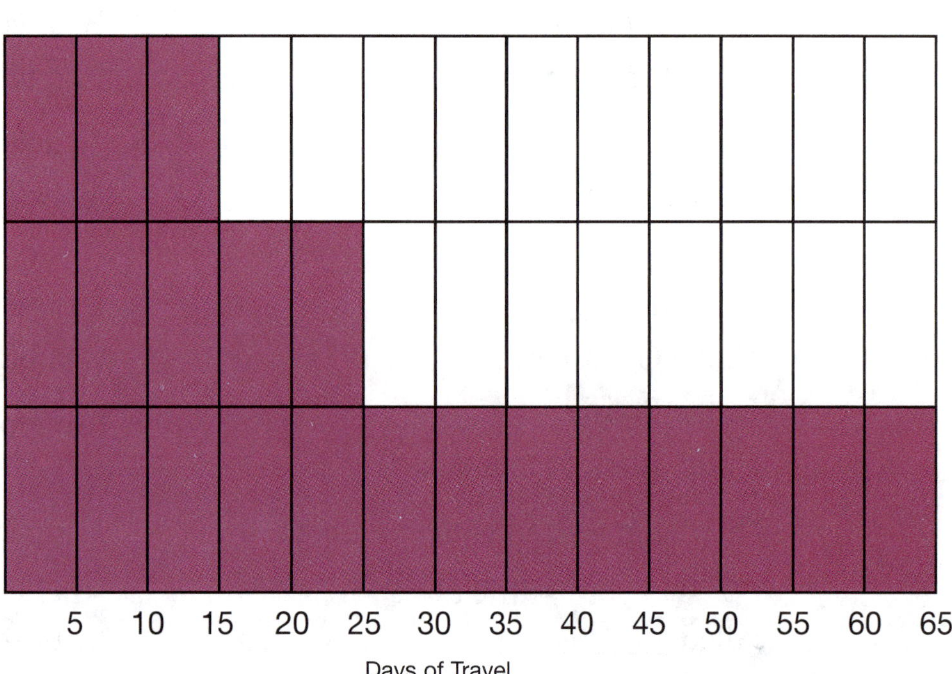

Use the bar graph to answer the questions.

1. How many days does it take to go the distance on foot? _______________

2. How many days does it take to go the distance on horseback? _______________

3. How much longer does it take to go on foot than on horseback? _______________

4. How long does it take to go by train? _______________

5. How much longer does it take to go on horseback than by train? _______________

6. How much longer does it take to go on foot than by train? _______________

Heritage Studies 3
Worktext—Chapter 3

With Lewis and Clark

Name_______________________________

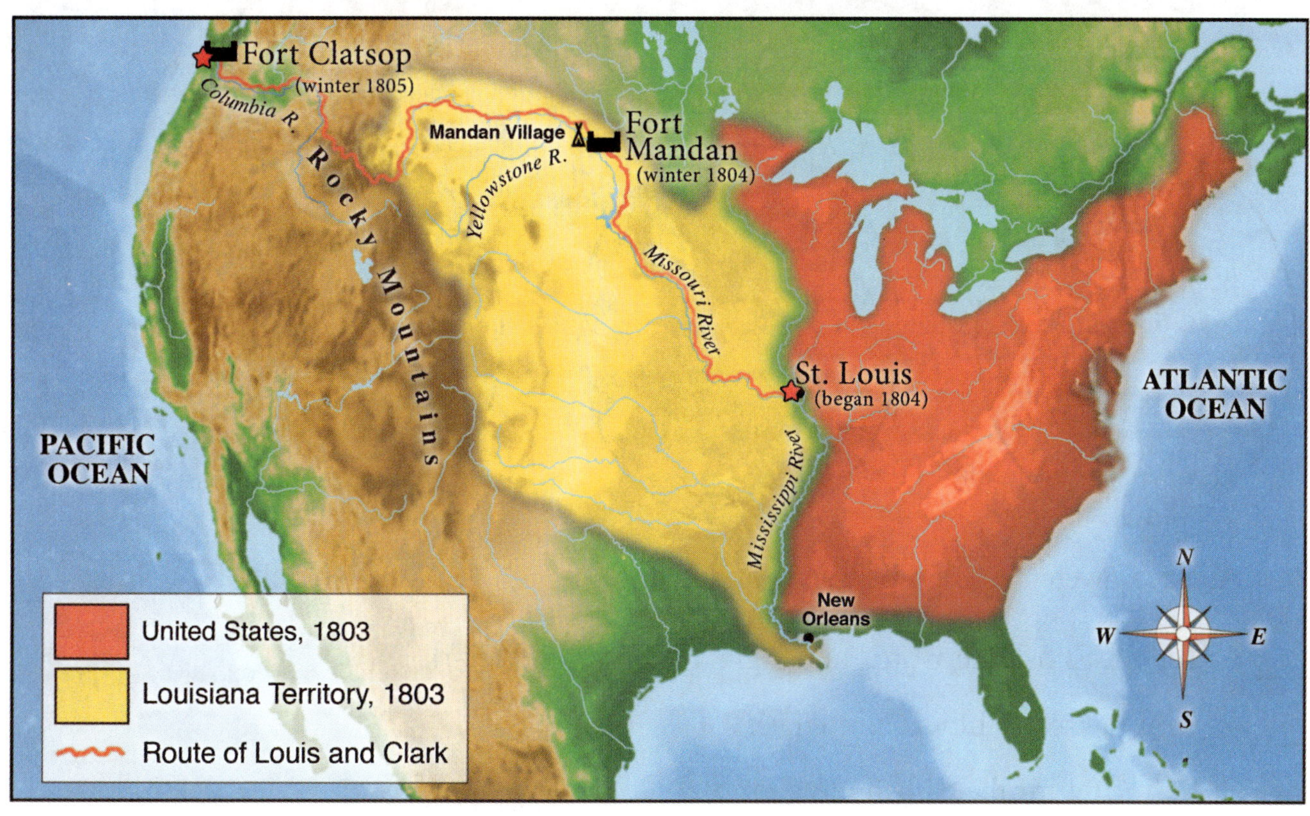

Lewis and Clark exploration

Use the map to answer the questions.

1. What land area did Thomas Jefferson purchase from Napoleon in 1803?

   ____

   _______________________ Territory

2. What two physical features on the map mark the boundaries of the Louisiana

   Territory? _______________________ Mountains, _______________________ River

3. What river did Lewis and Clark travel when they left St. Louis?

   _______________________ River

4. Lewis and Clark crossed the Shining Mountains. What is another name for

   these mountains? _______________________ Mountains

5. What ocean did Lewis and Clark reach? _______________________ Ocean

Name_______________________

Write the letter that matches each statement. Use Think About It and text pages 59-62.

A. Sacajawea   B. Lewis and Clark   C. Shoshone chief

______ 1. Taught Shoshone words and signs to Lewis and Clark

______ 2. Sold horses to Lewis and Clark

______ 3. Left gifts for the Shoshone people

______ 4. Shoshone woman who went on the exploration of the Louisiana Territory

______ 5. Was willing to help Lewis and Clark, but he did not give them land

______ 6. Knew herbs to use for medicine

______ 7. Supplied an old Indian guide to help Lewis and Clark cross the mountains

______ 8. Knew which plants and animals were good to eat

______ 9. Explored the Shining Mountains and reached the Pacific Ocean

______ 10. Returned to St. Louis after traveling two years, four months, and twelve days

Native Americans were often willing to be friendly to settlers, but they were not willing to give up their land to the settlers.

Heritage Studies 3
Worktext—Chapter 3

Journal Drawings

Name________________________________

William Clark made drawings like these in his journal. Read the labels. Draw a line from each drawing to the area on the map where that item might have been seen by Clark.

Pacific Coast canoe

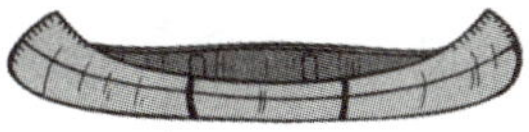

Northwest Indian arrow

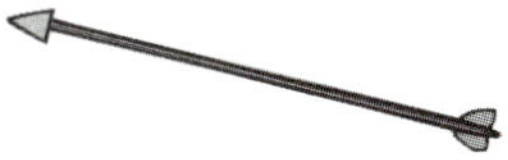

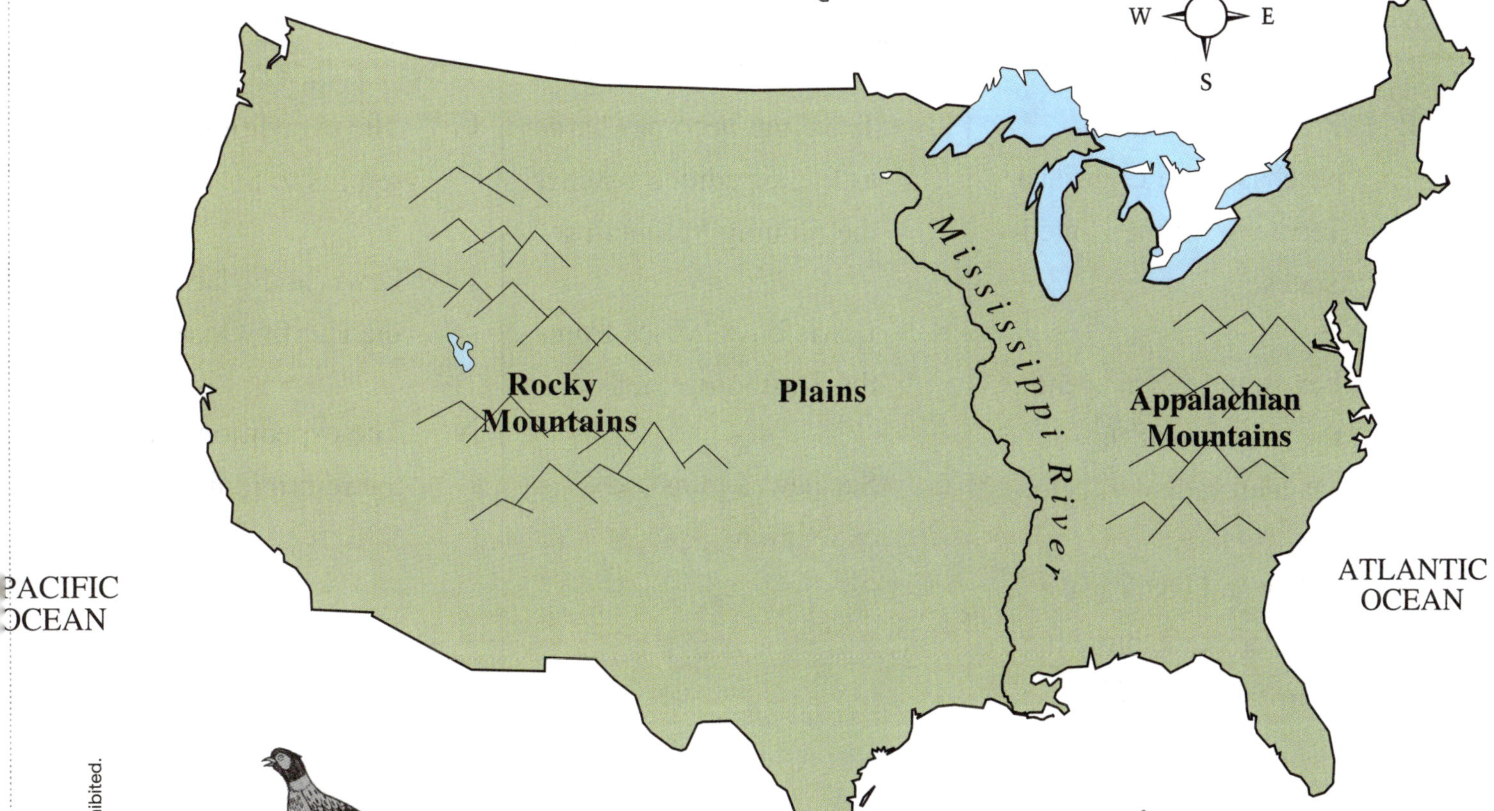

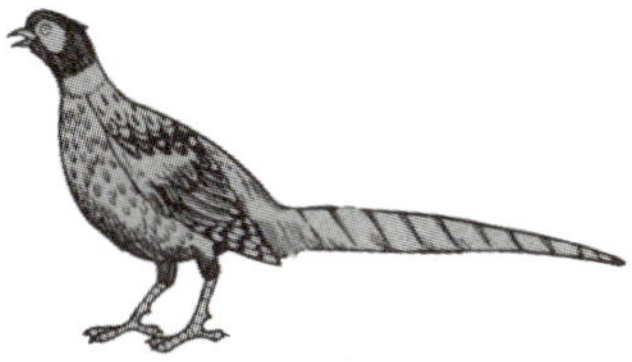

Rocky Mountain pheasant

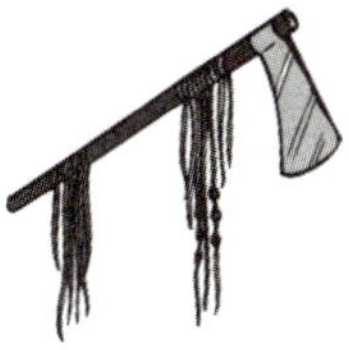

Plains Indian battle axe

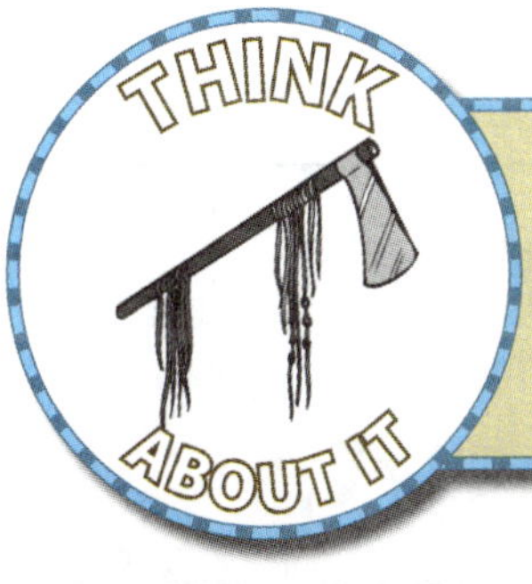

Lewis and Clark recorded the things they saw on their trip by keeping drawings and writings in **journals**.

Timeline

A. Read the events in each section. Think about the order in which each event occurred. Put the events in order on the timeline using the letter in front of each event.

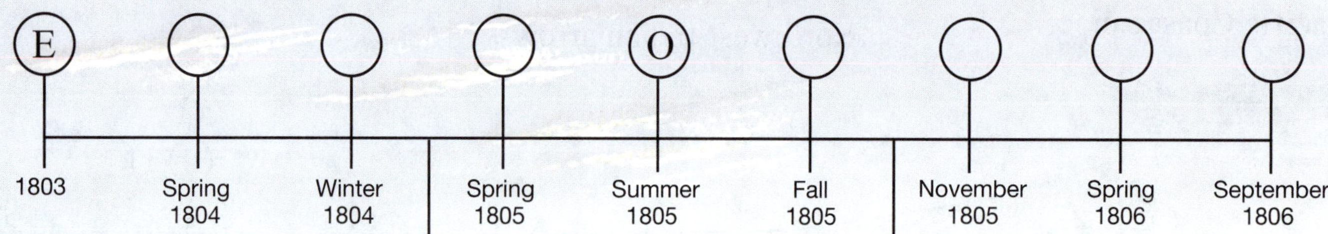

E				O				
1803	Spring 1804	Winter 1804	Spring 1805	Summer 1805	Fall 1805	November 1805	Spring 1806	September 1806

E President Jefferson purchases the Louisiana Territory for the United States.

P Lewis and Clark spend the winter near the Mandan Indian village.

X Lewis and Clark leave St. Louis to explore the Louisiana Territory.

O Traveling becomes harder as the expedition reaches the Shining Mountains.

R Lewis buys horses from the Shoshone chief.

L Sacajawea joins the expedition.

G The expedition returns to St. Louis.

I Lewis and Clark see the Pacific Ocean.

N The expedition starts the return journey.

B. Use the letters in the circles to form the answer to this statement:

Lewis and Clark traveled 8,000 miles ___ ___ ___ ___ ___ ___ ___ ___ ___

` the unfamiliar land of the Louisiana Territory.

Chapter Review

Complete the Chapter Review. Text pages are given with each question or section.
A. Write the letter of the answer in the blank.

______ 1. Lewis and Clark saw the Shining Mountains and _____. (60)

A. the Atlantic Ocean

B. the Arctic Ocean

C. the Pacific Ocean

______ 2. The Shoshone woman who helped Lewis and Clark on the trip was _____. (59)

A. Sacajawea

B. Mandan

C. Shining Mountains

______ 3. Lewis and Clark explored _____. (56)

A. the Florida Territory

B. the Louisiana Territory

C. the Ohio Territory

______ 4. Features such as mountains and lakes can be found on _____. (46)

A. road maps

B. city maps

C. physical maps

______ 5. President Jefferson directed the purchase of the Louisiana Territory from

_____. (56)

A. William Clark

B. Napoleon

C. Sacajawea

______ 6. One of the animals found in the Great

Forest was _____. (48)

A. the white-tailed deer

B. the bighorn sheep

C. the prairie dog

> *"Thou are worthy, O Lord, to receive glory and honour and power: for thou hast created all things, and for thy pleasure they are and were created."*
> **Revelation 4:11**

Name________________

B. Put a check mark next to each way that Sacajawea helped the men on the expedition (text pages 59–60).

☐ 7. She knew the herbs to use for medicine.

☐ 8. She knew which plants and animals were good to eat.

☐ 9. She gave the Native American lands to Lewis and Clark.

☐ 10. She helped the men buy horses from her people.

☐ 11. She kept a journal for Lewis and Clark.

☐ 12. She taught the men Shoshone words and signs.

C. Complete the map key according to the colors on the map and animal horn pictures (text pages 48–52).

Key	Land	Animals
Great Forest	◯	White-Tailed Deer ☐
Prairie	◯	Bison ☐
Rocky Mountains	◯	Bighorn Sheep ☐

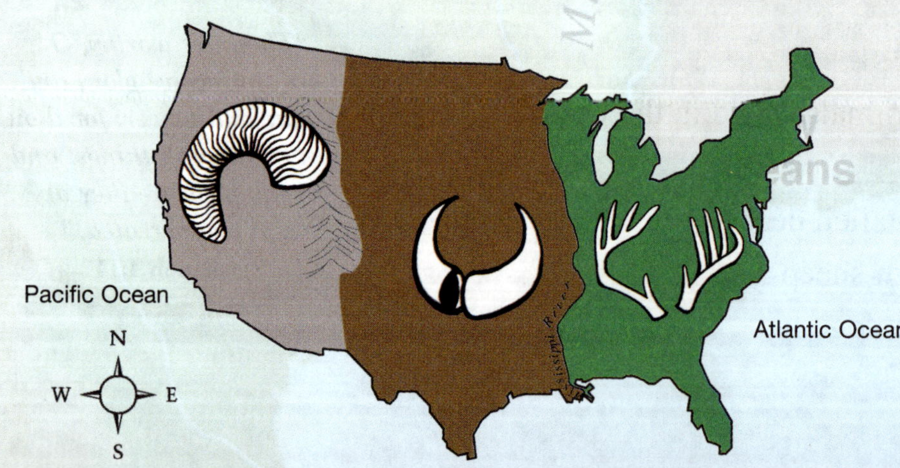

Famous Travels

Name______________________

1. Trace the routes Beckwourth traveled as your teacher reads the accounts of his first and second trips.
2. Use the map of Beckwourth's travels to answer the questions.

   A. Name three rivers that Beckwourth came in contact with on his first trip.

   B. At the time of Beckwourth's travels in the early 1800s, the land west of St Louis, Missouri, was not divided into states. If Beckwourth had made the same trip today, name three states he would have traveled through.

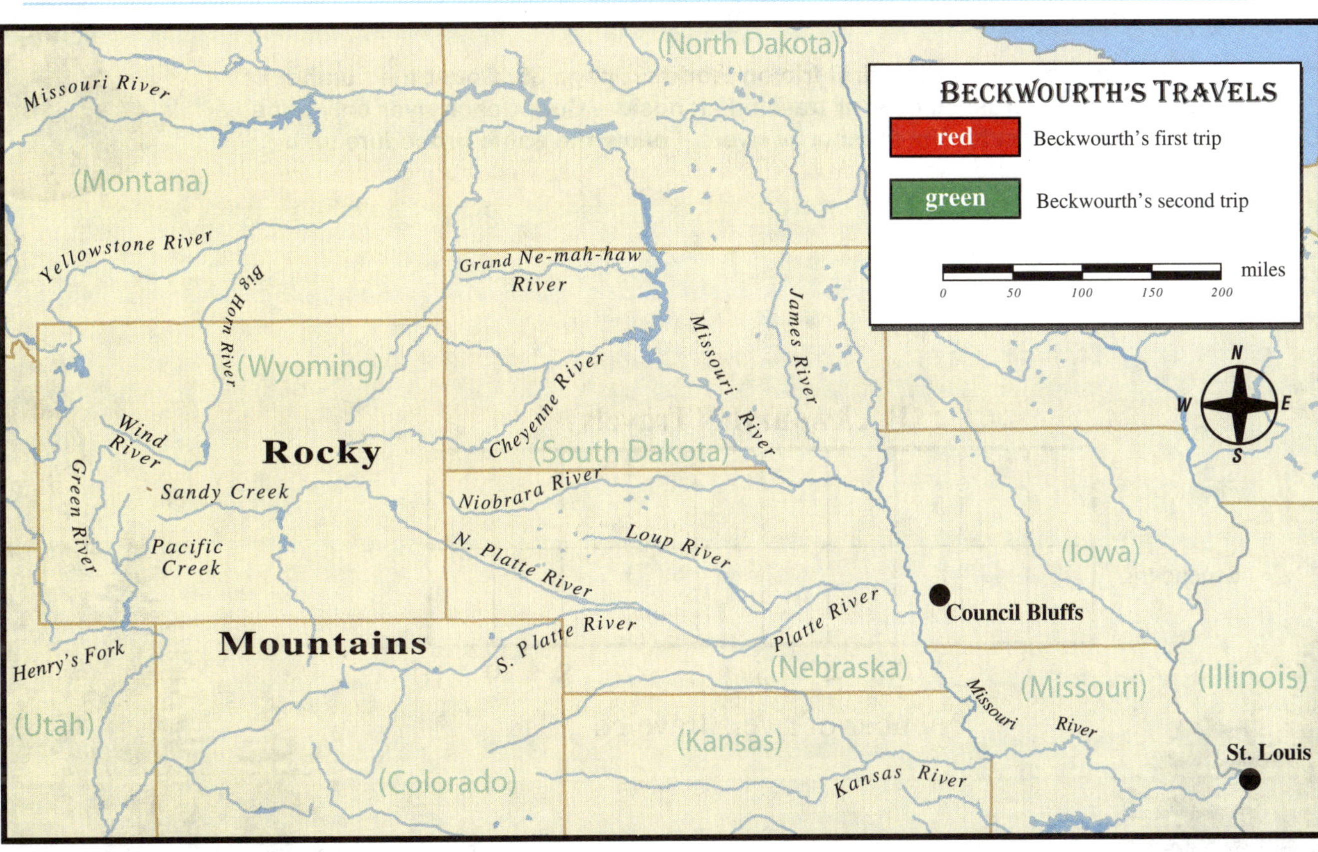

Long Hunters

Name_______________________________

A. Fill in the blanks using the word bank (text pages 64–67).

> arrows   Beckwourth   long   settlers   west

1. A _________________ hunter hunted for long periods of time and traveled long distances.

2. Long hunters encouraged people to travel _________________ by telling stories and giving advice.

3. James _________________ found a pass over the Rocky Mountains.

4. Some Indians shot _________________ at the settlers and burned their wagons.

5. The _________________ thought the land did not belong to anyone since no homes were on it.

B. Look at James Beckwourth's first trip on Worktext page 35. Count the number of labeled rivers he crossed over or traveled alongside. Count each river only once. Color the bar graph for the number of rivers. Follow the same procedure with Beckwourth's second trip.

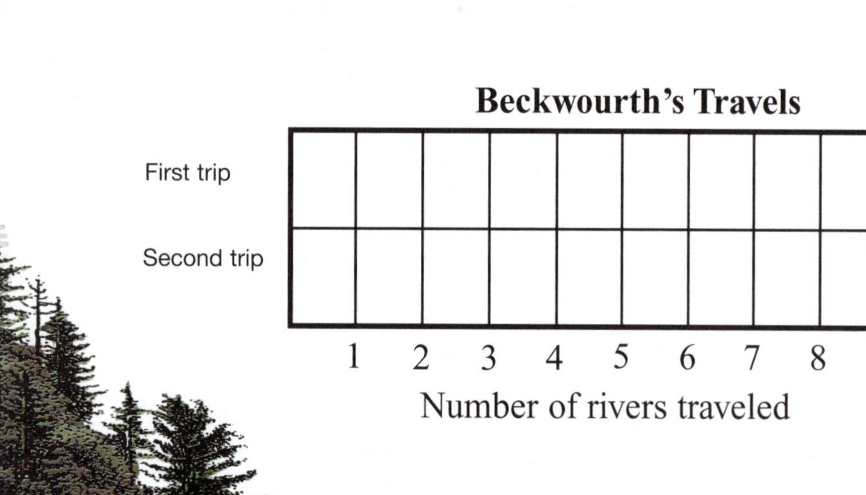

Beckwourth's Travels

	1	2	3	4	5	6	7	8	9	10
First trip										
Second trip										

Number of rivers traveled

Family's Route

Read the story of the Drake family. Draw a line on the map that traces the family's route.

Mr. and Mrs. Drake and their son Daniel left **Philadelphia, Pennsylvania**, on a rainy morning in 1810. They went by horse and wagon to **Pittsburgh, Pennsylvania**. There Mr. Drake bought a flatboat. The Drakes put all they owned on that boat, including the two horses and the wagon. Then they floated down the **Ohio River** to **Kentucky**. Once they landed in Kentucky, they went by wagon to **Lexington, Kentucky**. The people there told the Drakes that good land was open a little farther west. So the Drake family built a place to live a little west of the Lexington area.

Study Questions

Name___________________________

Dolley Madison wrote the following in a letter after the British burned much of Washington, DC, in the War of 1812: "I insist on waiting until the large picture of **Gen. Washington** is secured, and it requires to be unscrewed from the wall. . . . I have ordered the frame to be broken, and the canvass taken out."

A. Fill in the blanks using the word bank (text page 71).

American   English   France

1. England and ________________ were fighting against each other in a war.

2. English sailors who did not want to fight hid on ________________ ships.

3. English captains stopped American ships to search for ________________ sailors.

B. Fill in the blanks using the word bank (text pages 72–77).

Dolley   James   Key   treaty

4. ________________ Madison did not like having the English captains stopping American ships; he took the United States into war with England.

5. ________________ Madison rescued many important government treasures in Washington, DC, before the British burned most of the city.

6. Francis Scott ________________ wrote "The Star-Spangled Banner" on a British ship as he watched the American flag flying over Fort McHenry.

7. The War of 1812 ended in a ________________, an agreement between America and England.

Dolley Madison saved a full-length portrait of George Washington by Gilbert Stuart similar to this one pictured from the Gilbert Stuart collection.

Heritage Studies 3
Worktext—Chapter 4

Can You Still See the Flag?

Name_______________________________

Cast of Characters
(in order of appearance)

Three British soldiers

Dr. Beanes

Jailer

Two more British soldiers

Mr. Jansen

Mrs. Jansen

Colonel Skinner

Mrs. Lander

Mrs. Skinner

Mr. Francis Scott Key

President James Madison

British admiral

Scene One

(The scene takes place at night near the home of Dr. Beanes. The stage is quiet and dimly lit. From offstage three soldiers are heard singing. They enter singing and making noise. Dr. Beanes can be seen sleeping upstage.)

Soldiers: *(singing)* With a hey-ho, hey-nonny-ho! *(break off with laughing)*

Dr. Beanes: *(waking up)* What? What's the racket? *(getting up and calling out the window)* Hey! How about some quiet out there?

Soldier 1: *(loudly)* Quiet? You want quiet? Not us! *(beginning to bang around and yell)* Give the man some quiet, boys! *(The soldiers make all the noise they can.)*

Dr. Beanes: Please, men, be quiet! I have to get some sleep. *(A jailer enters, swinging keys and whistling.)* I say, jailer! Can you make these men be quiet?

Soldier 2: No, he can't. We're British soldiers!

Soldier 3: Let him try! I say he can't!

Jailer: I certainly can. Stand still, you three. Drop your guns and come with me! Do as I say, or I'll shoot!

(The soldiers do as they are told. They file off, followed by the jailer. Dr. Beanes falls asleep again.)

Name_______________________________

Scene Two

(The same night. Dr. Beanes is sleeping soundly. Two British soldiers enter.)

Soldier 4: Here's the house. *(loudly)* Dr. Beanes! Dr. Beanes! Get up! You are under arrest!

Dr. Beanes: What? Now what! Who's there?

Soldier 5: The soldiers of His Majesty, King George III. Come down and go with us!

Dr. Beanes: What's the charge? What have I been accused of?

Soldier 4: You were mean to some soldiers earlier tonight. Our admiral wants to see you. Come down, or we'll come get you.

Dr. Beanes: Oh, very well. This is ridiculous.

(Dr. Beanes comes to the soldiers, and they march him off.)

Scene Three

(It is early morning. Friends of the doctor are on the street: Mr. and Mrs. Jansen, Mrs. Lander, Colonel and Mrs. Skinner, and Mr. Francis Scott Key.)

Mr. Jansen: They took him right from his bed—no time to dress! They rode him off on a mule. Now he's on board the British ship.

Mrs. Jansen: Poor Dr. Beanes! He is always so kind and good to everyone! Why would they take him?

Colonel Skinner: No matter about that now. The thing to do is get him back!

Mrs. Lander: But how? The British ships have cannons and guns and so many soldiers. We can't get him back!

Mrs. Skinner: Maybe not with guns—but we have a better weapon.

Colonel Skinner: And what is that?

Mrs. Skinner: Words! And who is better with words than Mr. Key?

Mr. Key: Me? You think I can get Dr. Beanes back?

Colonel Skinner: My wife is right! You're the best speechmaker I ever heard. You can go talk to the admiral. He'll listen to you!

Mr. Key: I am willing to do anything to help Dr. Beanes. If you think I can do some good, I'll certainly try. I must ask the president first, though.

Scene Four

(Mr. Key and President Madison are talking as they look over the harbor toward the British ships.)

President Madison: It is the best way, Mr. Key. I appreciate your bravery.

Mr. Key: I am always glad to help a friend.

President Madison: I've asked Colonel Skinner to go with you.

Mr. Key: There's no need for that, Mr. President. I'm sure it'll be—

President Madison: No, Mr. Key. Colonel Skinner will go. God bless you both.

Scene Five

(On board the British ship the next day. Dr. Beanes is sitting in a chair with his hands tied. He does not look angry, just tired. Mr. Key, Colonel Skinner, and the admiral are talking together downstage. Two soldiers stand guard.)

Admiral: No, I will not hear any more. My men escaped from your jail and reported that this Dr. Beanes had them thrown in jail for nothing. I've heard enough!

Mr. Key: But what of Dr. Beanes's side of it? Has the British Empire given up its great tradition of fairness? Has its long history of law broken down?

Admiral: None of your fancy speeches, Mr. Key. The answer is no.

Mr. Key: *(looking at Colonel Skinner)* What can we say?

Colonel Skinner: *(stepping up to Mr. Key)* Show him these letters. They are from some British soldiers Dr. Beanes helped care for.

Name_________________________________

Mr. Key: Admiral, with your permission, I would like to show you some letters. If you will not believe me on the matter of Dr. Beanes's good character, perhaps you will believe your own men. *(He hands over the letters.)*

Admiral: *(opening a letter and reading from it)* "And in that time I found I owed my life to an American doctor, Dr. Beanes." Harumph. *(He opens another letter and reads.)* "But I was treated kindly by one American, a Dr. Beanes. He came many times to see whether I had all I needed—" Well, it seems I may have been wrong. Untie the doctor.

(A soldier unties Dr. Beanes. The doctor stands up, rubbing his wrists.)

Mr. Key: Thank you, Admiral. We'll be going.

Admiral: Not so fast. The doctor is free of charges, but you are not free to go. There is a battle beginning here, and I cannot have you going to your friends and giving out any secrets. No, you will wait aboard my ship until I say otherwise. *(He turns and strides off.)*

Mr. Key: I say! A battle! And we are to remain here?

Colonel Skinner: I shouldn't worry, my good fellow. See the flag flying over Fort McHenry? I dare say we shall see it there tomorrow as well!

Mr. Key: I pray that you are right, Colonel.

Scene Six

(The deck of a British ship. Mr. Key is pacing back and forth.)

Dr. Beanes: Come, Mr. Key. Please, come sit down and rest. You'll wear yourself out with all that pacing. And me with it, I fear.

Colonel Skinner: Yes, Mr. Key. We can do nothing but wait for morning.

Mr. Key: Oh! Did you see? In that bomb blast? The flag! Did you see it?

Dr. Beanes: I can't see anything. The smoke and mist are so thick.

Mr. Key: The American flag must not come down. Our defenses at Fort McHenry are strong enough, don't you think, Colonel?

Colonel Skinner: The fort is well defended. But these British guns are harder to hold out against than I thought.

Dr. Beanes: What will be, will be, my boy. Sit down now and wait. The sun will soon be coming up, and then we will see.

Mr. Key: There's another bomb bursting. Look! Can you see if the flag is still there?

Colonel Skinner: Can't see a thing. Wait. There—I saw it for a moment—truly I did.

Dr. Beanes: Praise be. Let us pray it is still there at sunrise.

Scene Seven

(Dr. Beanes is sleeping in a chair. Colonel Skinner is leaning against the rails of the ship. Mr. Key is straining to see the flag.)

Mr. Key: The sun is up enough, but I can't see the flag.

Colonel Skinner: If a breeze would stir, perhaps we could see it then.

Mr. Key: There it is! There it is! Praise be, the flag still flies! Wake up the doctor! The American flag is waving still!

(The admiral and two soldiers enter swiftly.)

Admiral: Put these Americans ashore! Then put to sea! Move!

(The admiral leaves on the opposite side of the stage as he entered. The soldiers stay and pantomime putting down a small boat into the water. The three Americans slap each other's backs and shake hands, saying together "hurrah." Mr. Key pulls out an envelope and writes on it.)

Dr. Beanes: What an adventure to tell my grandchildren!

Colonel Skinner: And what a story for the newspapers. Mr. Key, what are you doing?

Mr. Key: I'm putting this wondrous sight into a poem. "Oh, say, can you see by the dawn's early light . . ."

Pioneer Graph

A. Color the graph according to the following information:

1810: 1 million pioneers, 1820: 2 million pioneers, 1830: $3\frac{1}{2}$ million pioneers

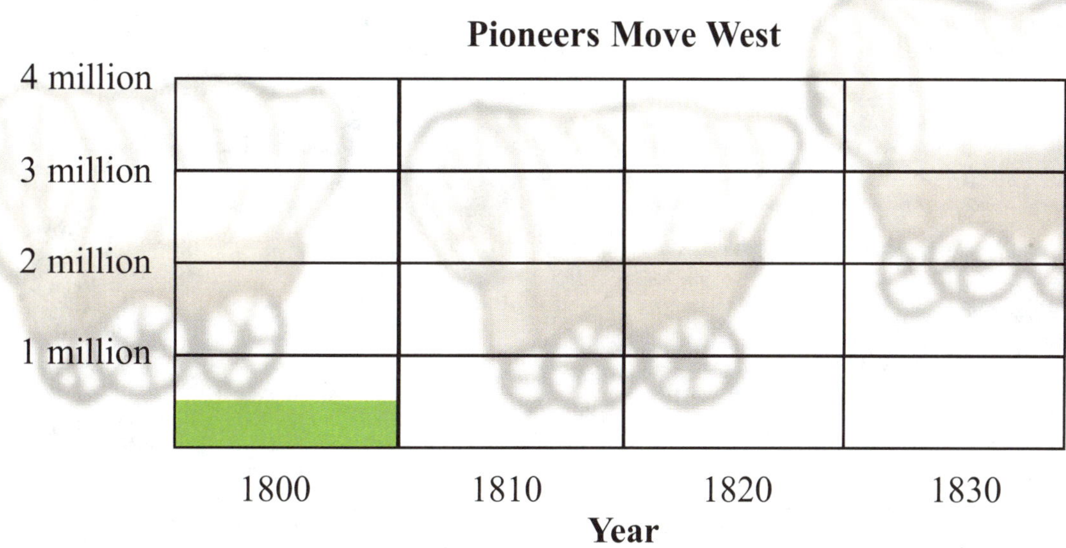

B. Use the graph to answer the questions.

1. How many pioneers had moved west in 1810? _______________

2. What year were the most pioneers living in the West? _______________

3. What year were there fewer than one million pioneers who had moved west?

____

____

4. What year would you have liked to travel? _______________ Tell why.

____

____

Trace Your Route

Name________________________

A. Draw the route you would take to go from Benborough to Fort Pine.

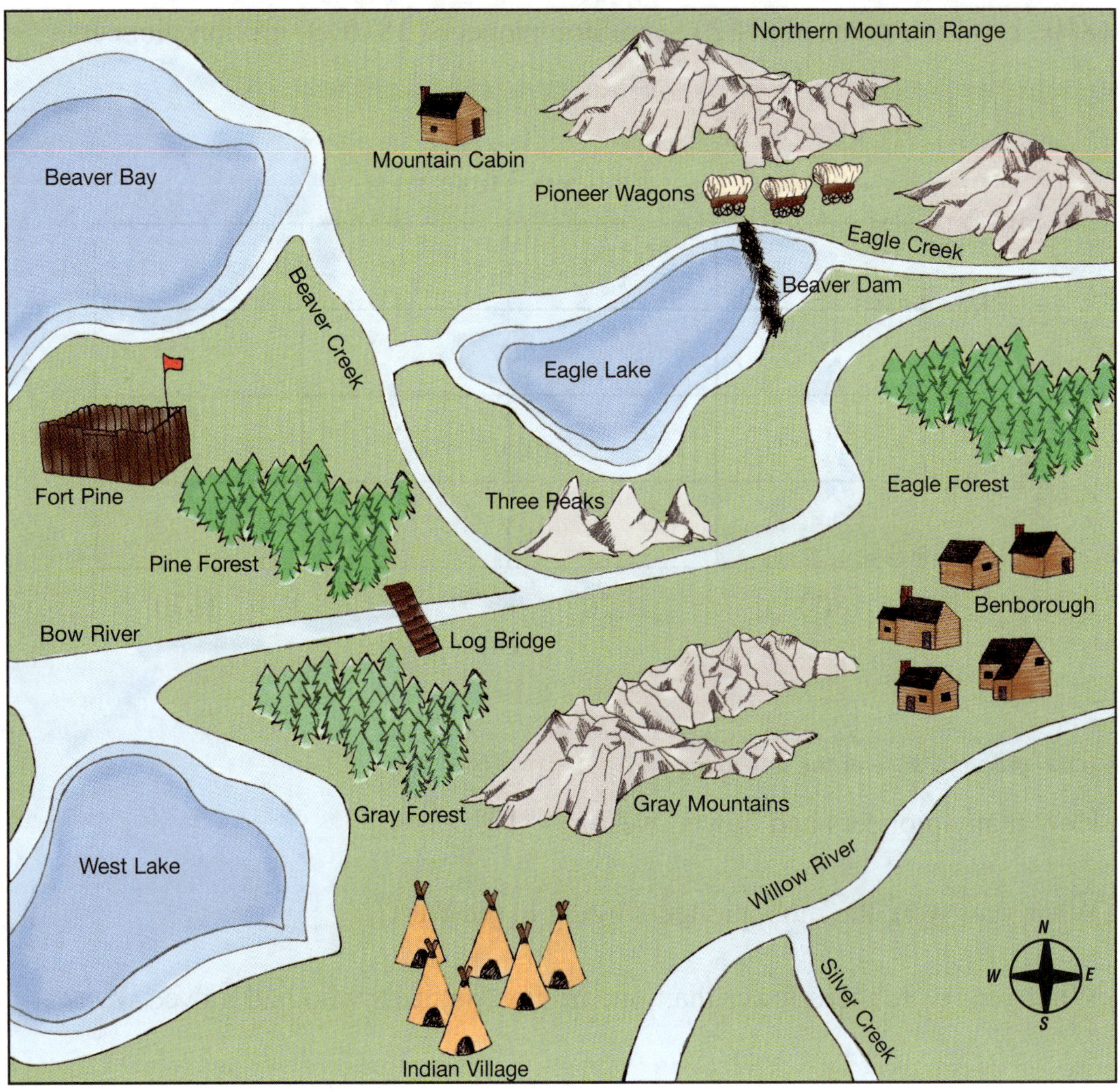

B. Write out the directions for your route.

Which Way Is West?

Name_______________________

Use the map to answer the questions.

1. What settlement is farthest east? ______________________

2. What creek will the pioneer wagons cross to go west? ______________________

3. What mountains are south of the Three Peaks? ______________________

4. Which is farther north: Fort Pine or Mountain Cabin? ______________________

5. Could a man from Fort Pine get to Indian Village without crossing water? ______

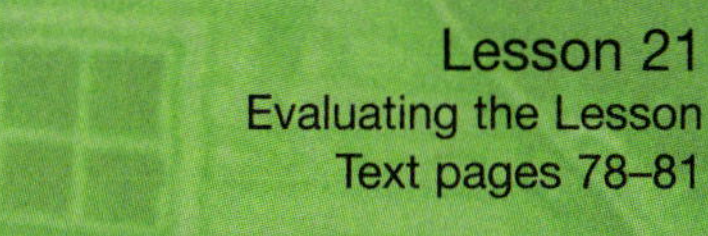

Landmarks

Circle the landmarks on the trail.

Heritage Studies 3
Worktext—Chapter 4

Study Questions

Name______________________________

A. Fill in the blanks using the word bank (text pages 80–81 and Think About It).

> Mormons   sin   Smith   Utah   works

1. Joseph _________________ believed that an angel gave him some teachings to add to the Bible.

2. The people who followed Joseph Smith were called the _________________.

3. The Mormons moved west across the prairies to settle in _________________.

4. Mormons believe that they can get to heaven by good _________________.

5. It is a _________________ to add extra teaching to the Bible.

B. Which group is described by each statement?
Mark an _X_ in the correct column (text page 82).

	American Settlers	American Government	American Indians
6. Wanted more land			
7. Followed the Trail of Tears			
8. Broke treaty or promise			
9. Forced to live on a reservation			

To change what God has said by adding anything to His Word is a sin. (Bible principle from Revelation 22:18–19)

Trail of Tears

Name_____________________________________

A. Use the map key to color the present-day states that the Cherokee walked through.

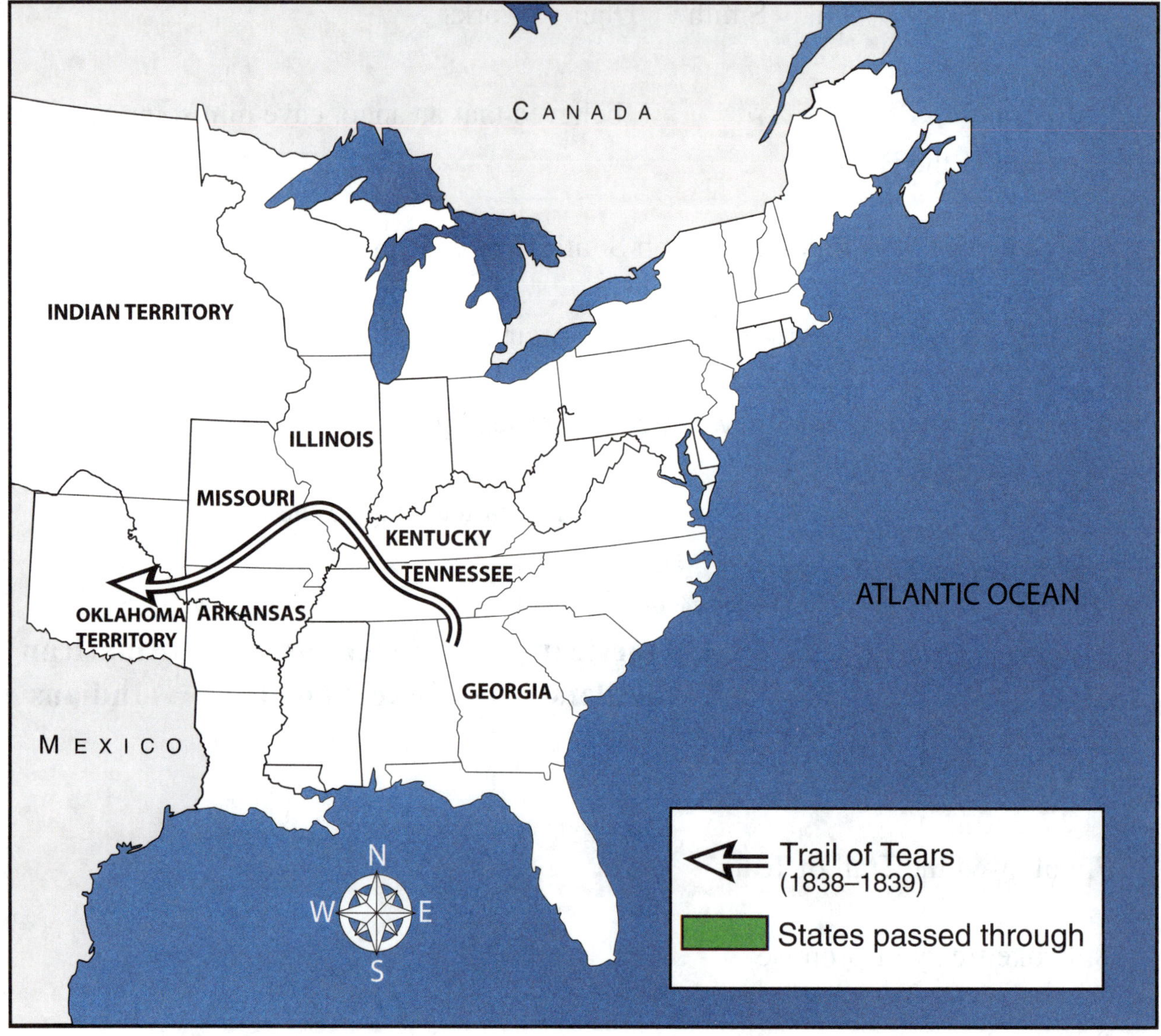

B. Use text page 82 and the map above to answer the questions.

1. What was the name of the journey the United States government forced the

   Cherokee to make? ____

2. Where were the Cherokee forced to go? _________________________________

3. Did the United States government keep its promise of food and help?

Heritage Studies 3
Worktext—Chapter 4

A Mountain Man

Most mountain men told tall tales. Some were partly true, and some were hardly true at all. But almost every story Jim Bridger told turned out to be true. Once he came back from the mountains and told about great fountains of steam bursting up from the ground and mud bubbling hot out of cracks in the earth. People laughed at him. Today we know about geysers and hot mudpots in Yellowstone National Park.

Some say that Bridger was the best hunter in the **Rocky** Mountains. He was a skilled trapper and hunter. Using his talents, he became a **guide**, helping people go west on the Oregon Trail.

Dr. Marcus Whitman went west with Bridger. When Bridger was shot in the back with an arrow, **Whitman** was able to remove it.

Dr. Whitman and his wife became pioneer missionaries to Native Americans living along the **Oregon** Trail. They also took in many children as their own, including Jim Bridger's daughter.

Fill in the blanks using the bold words in the story.

1. Jim Bridger was a skilled hunter in the

    _________________________ Mountains.

    ____

2. He became a _________________________,
   helping people go west on the Oregon Trail.

3. On his first trip west, Dr. Marcus

    ____

    _________________________ removed an

    arrow from Jim Bridger's back.

4. Dr. and Mrs. Whitman went west along the

    ____

    _________________________ Trail to become

    pioneer missionaries.

Name______________________________

A. Draw a line to match the meeting place with information (text pages 83–88).

rendezvous   1. In the summer families met for days of preaching services.

churches   2. Mountain men met to trade furs.

camp meeting   3. Circuit-riding preachers traveled many miles to preach.

B. Fill in the circle (text pages 83–88 and Think About It).

4. Missionaries were often ______.
   - ○ the first white people in a new place out west
   - ○ forced to wait for a wagon train

5. Camp meetings were ______.
   - ○ held in crowded cities
   - ○ preaching services held outside

6. John Sutter's Fort became famous ______.
   - ○ when gold was found
   - ○ when Sutter gave food to travelers

7. The "forty-niners" looked for ______.
   - ○ a pass over the Rockies
   - ○ gold in California

8. Thousands went to look for gold, ______.
   - ○ but most prospectors made little money
   - ○ and most prospectors struck it rich

9. Stephen Paxson traveled over one hundred thousand miles ______.
   - ○ to tell boys and girls about Jesus
   - ○ to find gold in California

The Bible went west too. **Stephen Paxson** traveled over one hundred thousand miles telling boys and girls about Jesus. Paxson taught children to read the Bible. He became the greatest Sunday school missionary in the history of the West.

Panning for Gold

Name_______________________________

Draw a line to match each description with the picture as your teacher reads Panning for Gold.

panning for gold

using a sluice

working a water wheel

mining for gold

It is better to be honest and have just a little than to be rich and have gained your riches dishonestly.

(Bible principle from Proverbs 16:8)

Name_______________________________

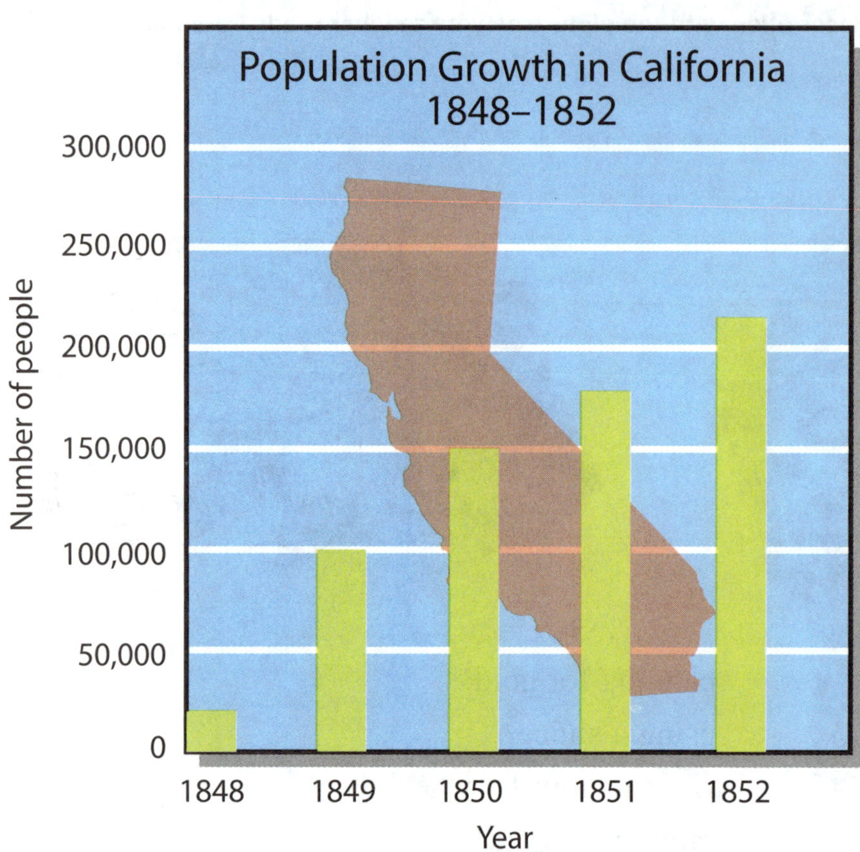

Use text pages 86–88 and the graph to answer the questions.

1. Gold was discovered in 1848 at Sutter's Mill. What was the population of California in 1848?
   - ○ about 20,000
   - ○ about 700,000

2. What was the population the next year, 1849?
   - ○ 250,000
   - ○ 100,000

3. What did the gold seekers call themselves?
   - ○ forty-niners
   - ○ fifty-nifties

4. Which statement is true about people looking for gold in California?
   - ○ People started families and became successful farmers.
   - ○ Most people left when they did not find gold.

5. What brought miners to California?
   - ○ gold rush or gold
   - ○ family farms

Name________________________

A. James Beckwourth   B. James Madison   C. Stephen Paxson   D. Joseph Smith

A. Look at the pictures above. Write the letter of the answer in the blank.

______ 1. Who was the greatest Sunday school missionary of the West?

______ 2. Who was the first Mormon leader? (80)

______ 3. Who found a pass over the Rocky Mountains? (66)

______ 4. Who took the United States into war against England? (72)

B. Write the letter of the answer in the blank.

A. "The Star-Spangled Banner"   C. War of 1812

B. Trail of Tears   D. "forty-niners"

______ 5. What prospectors came to California in search of gold? (88)

______ 6. When did the United States win its rights with a treaty? (77)

______ 7. What says the American flag continues to fly over Fort McHenry? (75)

______ 8. What was the difficult journey westward by the Cherokee? (82)

C. Write the letter of the answer in the blank.

A. Mormons   C. Native Americans

B. missionaries   D. United States government

______ 9. Who did not keep a treaty with the Cherokee? (82)

______ 10. Who added to God's Word and believed in good works to go to heaven? (81)

______ 11. Who were often the first people to go west and tell people about Christ? (83)

______ 12. Who burned wagons because white men were crossing the Plains? (67)

Name_______________________________

D. Fill in the blanks using the word banks.

> Cherokee   government   reservation

13. Settlers forced the _______________ from their land. (82)

14. The United States _______________ promised food and help for the Cherokee. (82)

15. A place set aside for Native Americans is a _______________. (82)

> circuit-riding   days   love

16. Missionaries went west to tell Indians about Christ's _______________. (84)

17. _______________ preachers traveled from town to town. (84)

18. Camp meetings were held outside and lasted several _______________. (85)

E. Fill in the circle.

19. In 1848 gold was discovered in _____. (87)   ○ Sutter's Mill   ○ New Mexico

20. Many men hurried to California in the gold rush of _____. (88)

  ○ 1812   ○ 1849

21. California became famous for _____. (88)   ○ vegetables and fruit   ○ industry

22. The pioneers _____. (67)   ○ wanted more land   ○ deserved more land

23. It is a sin to _____. (80)   ○ add to God's Word   ○ read God's Word

24. The Mormons settled in a place we now know as _____. (81)

  ○ California   ○ Utah

Name_______________________

Jesus told many stories that helped people understand truths from God's Word. These stories are called **parables**. Jesus used **parables** in His teaching.

A. Fill in the blanks using the word bank.

> fable   parable   stories

1. We can learn about people from long ago by their _______________.

2. A Bible story used by Jesus that teaches a lesson is a _______________.

3. A story that teaches a lesson through the things animals do is a _______________.

B. Read the story parts and titles. In each blank, write *P* for parable or *F* for fable.

_______ 4. The Birds, practicing in the treetops, did not brag like the Animals. Eagle Chief told the other Birds, "We may not be as big and strong as the Animals, but we will play hard. We must do our best."

_______ 5. "Behold, a sower went forth to sow; and when he sowed, some seeds fell by the way side, and the fowls came and devoured them up: Some fell upon stony places, where they had not much earth." (Matthew 13:3–5)

_______ 6. A Lion was awakened from sleep by a Mouse running over his face. Rising up angrily, he caught him and was about to kill him when the Mouse sadly begged, "If you would only spare my life, I would be sure to repay your kindness." The Lion laughed and let him go.

_______ 7. The Prodigal Son (Luke 15:11–32)

_______ 8. Once upon a time a Frog left his home in the marsh and told all the Beasts that he was a learned doctor. He knew the use of medicine and was able to heal all diseases. A Fox asked him, "How can you pretend to heal others when you are unable to heal your own lame walk and wrinkled skin?"

_______ 9. The Pharisee and the Tax Collector (Luke 18:9–14)

Apples of Gold

Name_________________________

A. Look up Proverbs 25:11 in your Bible. Use the verse to complete the page.

1. What fruit is mentioned in this verse? _______________________

2. What is unusual about the apples? _______________________

3. Do you think Solomon thought the gold apples were pleasing? _______

B. Pleasant words are like gold apples. Inside the apple outlines, write nice words that you could say.

Johnny Appleseed

Name_______________________________

Complete the crossword puzzle using the word banks.

Across

3. Johnny paddled a _____ down the Ohio River.

4. The town of _____ was as far west as most people went during Johnny's day.

7. Johnny Appleseed wore a _____ on his head.

8. Johnny called the stories he read from the Bible "the good news from _____."

Down

1. All the wagons passing Johnny Appleseed's farm seemed to be going _____ (direction).

2. Johnny grew apples on his _____.

3. Johnny Appleseed's real name was John _____.

4. Johnny Appleseed wore a _____ sack as a shirt.

5. Johnny carried a big black _____ everywhere.

6. An exaggerated story about a real person is called a _____.

canoe
heaven
Pittsburgh
pot

Bible
Chapman
farm
legend
potato
west

Name________________________

A. Fill in the blanks using the word bank.

| apple   authors   Bible   cherry   Grimm   legend |

_____________ 1. An exaggerated story about a real person is a _____.

_____________ 2. George Washington did not cut down the _____ tree.

_____________ 3. Johnny Appleseed cared about planting _____ seeds.

_____________ 4. Johnny died in a little apple orchard in Indiana, his _____ lying open by his side.

_____________ 5. Jakob and Wilhelm _____ were two of the first people to collect stories in books.

_____________ 6. People that write stories are called _____.

B. Read the story parts and titles. In each blank, write *legend* or *folktale* for the type of story.

Jakob and Wilhelm Grimm collected stories and put them in books.

_____________ 7. People thought Johnny Appleseed was crazy, and you might have thought so too if you had seen him. The longer he stayed in the wilderness, the funnier Johnny looked.

_____________ 8. Soon Deer comes to the water. He needs a drink after he hard run. "Hey, Deer," Alligator calls, "Them things they call hounds is very good to eat. They easy to catch and they got no horn to scratch my throat when I swallow."

_____________ 9. "Sleeping Beauty"

_____________ 10. "Hansel and Gretel"

Tall Tale

Name_______________________________

A. If the statement is true, circle *True*. If the statement is false, circle *False*.

True   False   1. Tall tales were heard only in America.

True   False   2. Tall tales do not have outright lies.

B. If the statement agrees with "The Best Steel Man," put an *X* in the Tall Tale column. If the statement does not agree, put an *X* in the Does Not Agree column.

In the tall tale "The Best Steel Man," Joe Magarac stood taller than the trees.

Tall Tale	Does Not Agree

3. Steve held a contest to find the strongest man to marry his daughter.

4. Steve Mestrovich had the prettiest daughter in all the world.

5. Everybody knew Joe Magarac.

6. Joe's hands were as big as shovels, and his arms and legs were as big around as oak trees.

7. Pete Pussick was just as strong as Joe Magarac.

8. Joe Magarac squeezed the steel between his fingers and made eight rails at a time.

Children enjoy listening to fables, legends, folktales, and tall tales.

Chapter Review

Name________________________

A. Write *true* if the statement is true. If the statement is false, write the correct word to make the statement true.

___________________ 1. A <u>parable</u> is a story Christ used to teach a lesson. (91)

___________________ 2. A parable is usually about <u>animals</u>. (91)

___________________ 3. The main characters in a fable are <u>animals</u>. (91)

___________________ 4. Johnny Appleseed cared about planting <u>cherry</u> trees. (97)

___________________ 5. The <u>Happy</u> brothers collected stories in books. (100)

___________________ 6. Tall tales are full of <u>lies</u>. (104)

___________________ 7. Tall tales were heard only in <u>England</u>. (104)

B. Read the story parts and titles. In each blank, write *parable, fable, legend, folktale,* or *tall tale* for the type of story.

___________________ 8. Johnny spent the rest of his days in the wilderness planting apple trees. Forty years after he left Pittsburgh, he died in a little apple orchard in Indiana, his Bible lying open by his side. (95–99)

___________________ 9. The Prodigal Son (Luke 15:11–32) (91)

___________________ 10. Paul Bunyan set up his logging camp with the greatest crew of loggers that has ever existed. He had so many men in his camp that in one of his bunkhouses, the bunk beds rose in the air thirty-seven beds high. (104)

___________________ 11. "Hansel and Gretel" (101)

___________________ 12. With a little sneer, Fox called up to the now unhappy Crow, "Thank you, Mistress Crow, but here's some advice for you. Never trust a flatterer." (91)

The Northeast

Name_______________________

Match each state with its capital and shape. Use worktext page 74.

Vermont

Maine

New Hampshire

Concord

Montpelier

Massachusetts

Connecticut

Rhode Island

New York

New Jersey

Pennsylvania

Delaware

Maryland

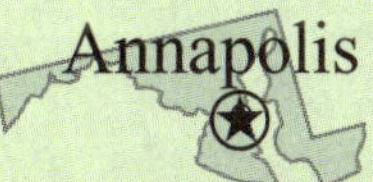

Portland Head Lighthouse, Portland, Maine

Central Park, New York City, New York

The Capitol Building, Washington, DC

The Northeast

Name______________________________

Fill in the blanks using the word bank.

Atlantic	harbor	Native	Separatists	Vermont

1. ________________________ were the first people to come from England to the Northeast region.

2. ________________________ Americans lived in the Northeast region before the English people came.

3. The ________________________ Ocean lies next to the Northeast region.

4. A ________________________ is a safe place for ships to dock.

5. ________________________ means "green mountain" in French.

STATE SMART SUPPLEMENT

Select one state from the Northeast region. Use reference materials to fill in the blanks.

State name: ________________________

State nickname: ________________________

State bird: ________________________

State tree: ________________________

State flower: ________________________

Name of one river in the state: ________________________

The Southeast

Match each state with its capital and shape. Use worktext page 74.

Kentucky

West Virginia

Virginia

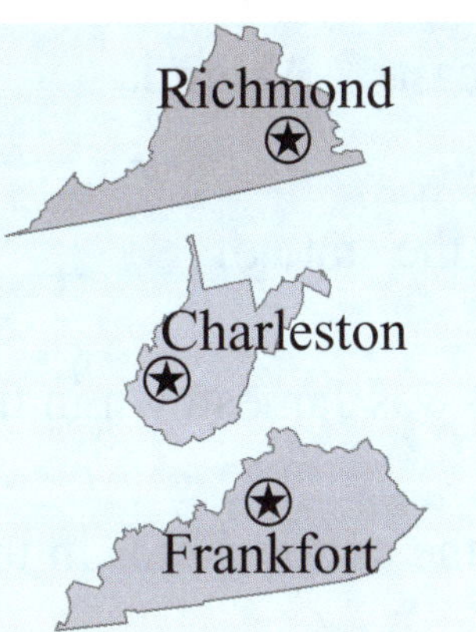

Tennessee

North Carolina

South Carolina

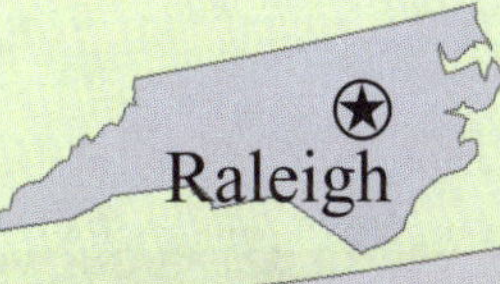

Georgia

Alabama

Florida

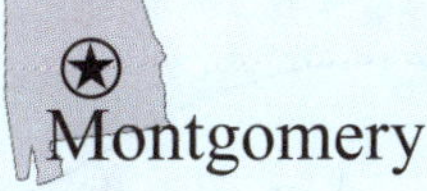
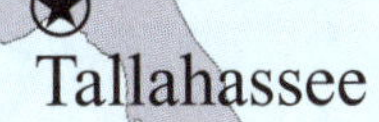

Mississippi

Louisiana

Arkansas

Tomb of the Unknowns, Arlington National Cemetery, Arlington, Virginia

From the Blue Ridge Parkway, North Carolina

The Everglades, Florida

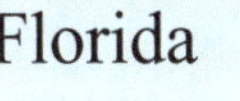

The Southeast

Name_______________________________

A. Fill in the blanks using the word bank.

| South Carolina | Southeast | Virginia |

1. The Charleston harbor is in the state of _________________.

2. The first English settlement was Jamestown in the state of _________________.

3. Long ago slaves worked in the cotton fields in the _________________.

B. Look at text page 112. List three tribes that lived in the Southeast.

____

____

STATE SMART SUPPLEMENT

Select one state from the Southeast region. Write the name of the state and its capital. Use reference materials to draw and color its flag.

____

____

The Middle West

Name________________________

Match each state with its capital and shape. Use worktext page 74.

Michigan

Ohio

Indiana

Illinois

Missouri

Iowa

Wisconsin

North Dakota

Minnesota

Nebraska

Kansas

South Dakota

Indianapolis

Columbus

Lansing

Springfield

Des Moines

Jefferson City

St. Paul

Madison

Bismarck

Pierre

Lincoln

Topeka

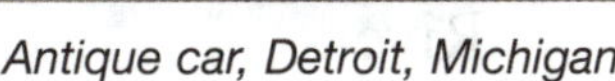

Antique car, Detroit, Michigan

Gateway Arch, St. Louis, Missouri

A field in the Midwest region

The Middle West

Name_______________________

A. Fill in the blanks using the word bank.

| Lewis | Midwest | Mississippi | Missouri |

1. Another name for the Middle West region is the ________________.

2. The boundary between Iowa and Nebraska is the ________________ River.

3. The western border for Wisconsin and Illinois is the ________________ River.

4. The two explorers that saw much of this region were ________________ and Clark.

B. Most of the Great Lakes are in this region.
   Look at text page 117. Name the five Great Lakes.

____

____

____

STATE SMART SUPPLEMENT

Using the map on text page 117, find the Midwest state that borders the most other Midwest states. Fill in the blanks.

State name: ________________

Six border states:

1. ________________   4. ________________

2. ________________   5. ________________

3. ________________   6. ________________

River borders: 1. ________________   2. ________________

Name_______________________________

A. Match each statement with the correct region by writing the abbreviation in the blank.

_______ 1. The first lasting English settlement was in this region.

_______ 2. German farmers and Quakers came to this region.

_______ 3. The Separatists settled in this region.

_______ 4. Lewis and Clark were among the first white men to see this region.

_______ 5. The Charleston harbor is located in this region.

NE Northeast

SE Southeast

MW Midwest

B. Fill in the blanks using the word banks.

| Northeast | Southeast | Midwest |

6. Maine is a part of the _______________ region.

7. Ohio is a part of the _______________ region.

8. Four of the Great Lakes are a part of the _______________ region.

9. The Atlantic Ocean borders the _______________ and Southeast regions.

10. Slaves worked in the cotton fields of the _______________ region.

| harbor | Missouri | six |

11. The United States can be divided into _______________ groups of states.

12. A safe place for ships to dock is a _______________.

13. The _______________ River forms the boundary between Iowa and Nebraska.

The Southwest

Name_______________________________

A. Match each state with its capital and shape. Use worktext page 74.

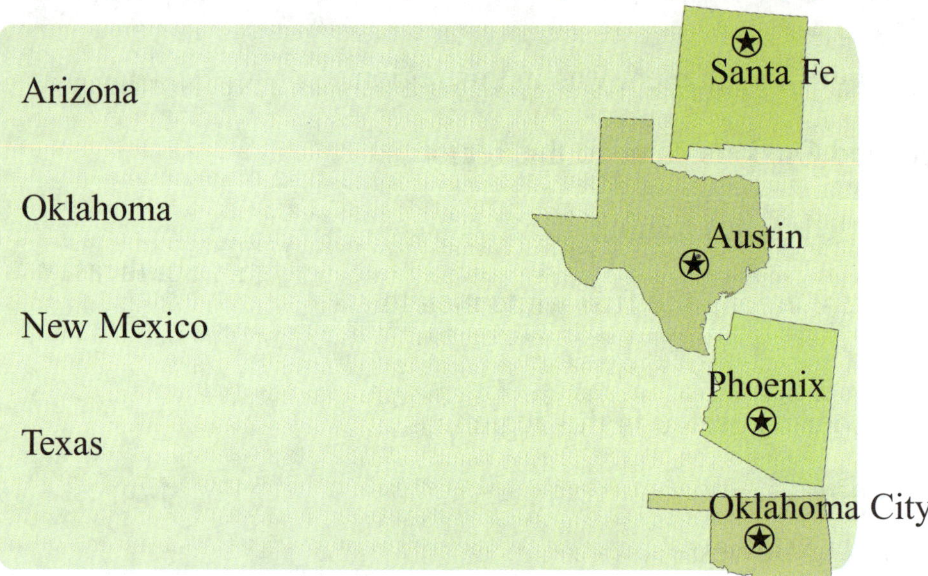

Oil rig, Texas

B. Fill in the blanks using the word bank.

| Coronado | irrigation | Santa Fe |

1. Spanish explorer _______________
   looked for the Seven Cities of Gold.
2. The oldest capital city in the United States is

   _______________, New Mexico.

Grand Canyon, Arizona

3. The Southwest depends on _______________ to water crops.

STATE SMART SUPPLEMENT

Spanish has enriched our language. Use your resources
to match the Spanish and English words.

¡Buenos días!   thank you

amigo   friend

gracias   party

fiesta   Good morning!

Piñata

Heritage Studies 3
Worktext—Chapter 6

The Rocky Mountain Region

A. Match each state with its capital and shape. Use worktext page 74.

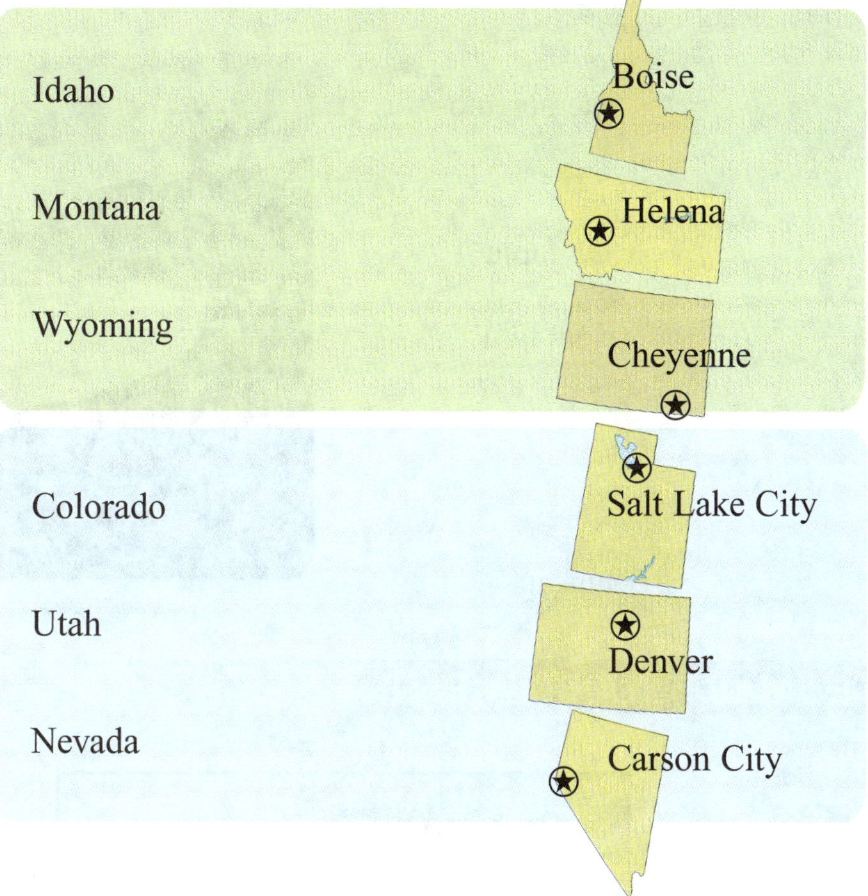

Glacier National Park, Montana

Elk, Yellowstone National Park, Wyoming

B. Fill in the blanks using text page 122 and Think About It.

1. The Rocky Mountain and Pacific regions together are called the ________________.

2. The ________________ ________________ kept people from settling in the West for many years.

3. Wyoming's famous tourist attraction is ________________ National Park.

4. The most famous geyser is called Old ________________.

Wyoming's famous tourist attraction is Yellowstone National Park, which has geysers, mudpots, and hot springs. The most famous geyser is called Old Faithful.

The Pacific Region

Match each state with its capital and shape. Use worktext page 74.

Hawaii

Oregon

Alaska

California

Washington

★ Sacramento

★ Olympia

★ Honolulu

★ Salem

Juneau ★

Maui, Hawaii

STATE SMART SUPPLEMENT

Use the grid map to answer the questions. For example: Follow letter D down the grid; follow number 4 across the grid to locate Sacramento.

Name the state pictured ______________________

on the grid map. ______________________

What interesting places to visit are indicated by each grid location?

E10 ______________________

C1 ______________________

C5 ______________________

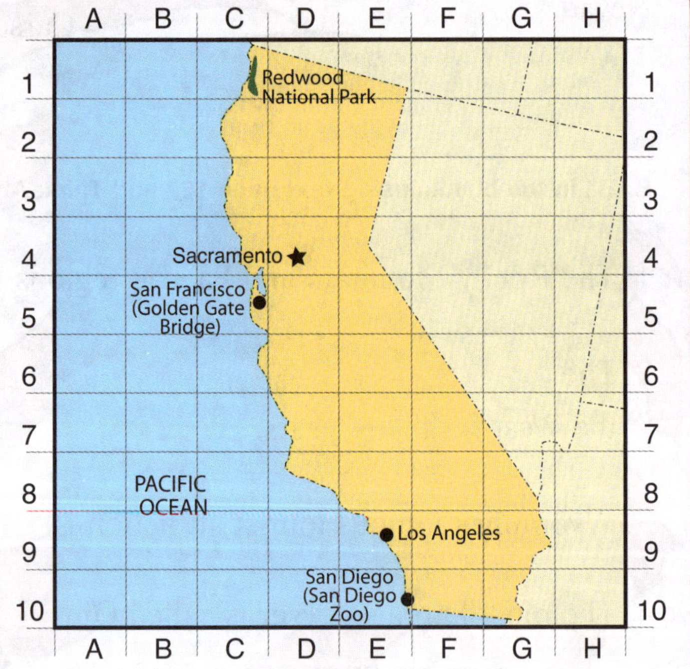

Name____________________

Match each statement with the correct region by writing the abbreviation in the blank.

______ 1. This region had mountains that kept pioneers from settling in the West.

______ 2. Gold was found in Sutter's Creek, a town in this region.

______ 3. The dry areas in this region depend on irrigation to water crops.

______ 4. Santa Fe, the oldest capital city in the United States, is in this region.

______ 5. The Rocky Mountains, along with *this region*, make up the West.

______ 6. Captain James Cook sailed to the islands in this region.

______ 7. In this region the explorer Coronado looked for the Seven Cities of Gold.

______ 8. Colorado is in this region.

Grid Map: Follow letter F down the grid; follow number 3 across the grid to locate the capital of Colorado. Use the grid locations to find other cities in Colorado. Write the name of each city.

The capital is _________________. (F3)

B8 _________________

G6 _________________

F2 _________________

A4 _________________

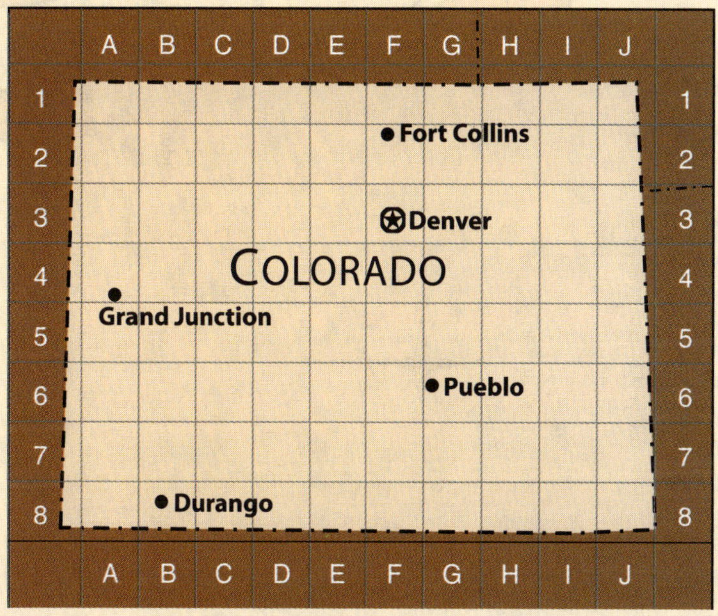

The United States

Name_______________________

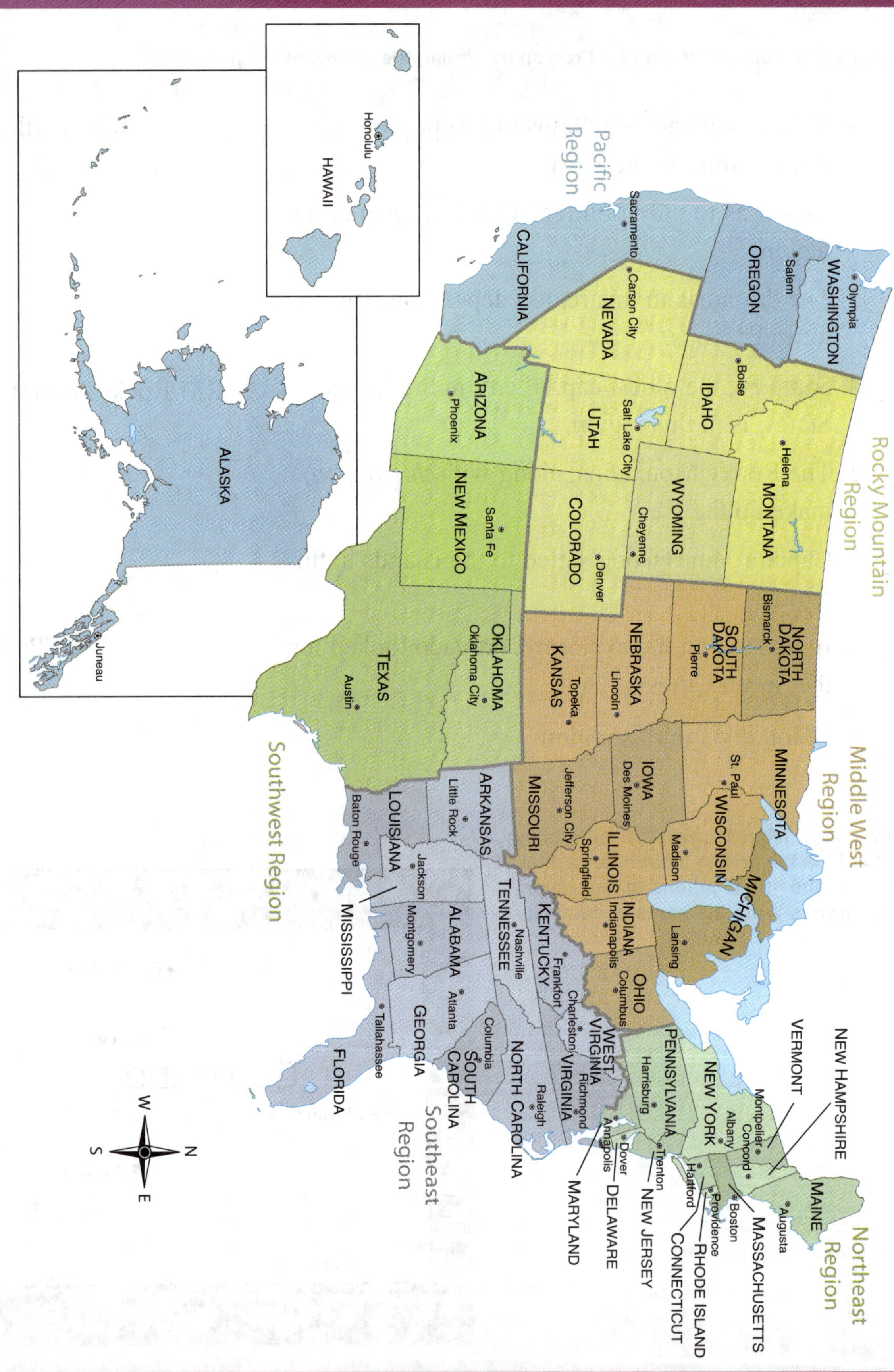

Chapter Review

Name_______________________

A. Mark an *X* in the correct column.

Northeast **Southeast** **Midwest**

1. Lewis and Clark explored this region. (116)

2. Cotton fields were in this region. (115)

3. Separatists settled here. (111)

4. The Revolutionary War began here. (111)

5. Most of the Great Lakes are here. (117)

6. Maine is located in this region. (111)

7. Ohio is in this region. (117)

8. The first lasting English settlement began here. (114)

Pacific **Rocky Mountains** **Southwest**

9. This region depends on irrigation. (120)

10. The settlers were stopped here. (122)

11. Colorado is in this region. (122)

12. Coronado looked for gold here. (119)

13. Gold was found here at Sutter's Creek. (122)

14. Santa Fe, New Mexico, is in this region. (120)

Name_______________________

B. Fill in the blanks using the word bank.

Atlantic	harbor	Midwest	Missouri	West	Wyoming

________________ 15. What ocean lies next to the Northeast region? (111)

________________ 16. Yellowstone National Park is in what state?

________________ 17. What river lies between Iowa and Nebraska? (117)

________________ 18. Where is a safe place for ships to dock? (113)

________________ 19. What are the Rocky Mountain and Pacific regions together called? (122)

________________ 20. What is another name for the Middle West? (116)

STATE SMART SUPPLEMENT

Choose one of the following options. Use your reference materials to draw a picture.

- **A geyser** "blowing off steam." See Yellowstone National Park, Wyoming.

- **The mountains and canyons** you might see in Colorado. The Spanish word *Colorado* means "colored red."

An Invention

A. Match each quotation with the person most likely to have said it by writing the letter in the blank.

> A. Eli Whitney   C. a Northern factory worker
> B. a slave   D. a Southern plantation owner

_______ 1. "There must be a way to make cotton seed free.
Perhaps a new powered machine is the key."

_______ 2. "To bed after dark and then up with the sun,
Will all of my master's work ever be done?"

_______ 3. "See all those people at work in my field?
This year my cotton should have a great yield!"

_______ 4. "I might work like a slave, but my wages I earn.
And my children go to school, read books, and learn."

_______ 5. "With my new invention, the South will be set.
More cotton they'll plant, and more money they'll get."

Eli Whitney invented the cotton gin, which removed cotton seeds.

B. Fill in the blanks using the word bank.

> cotton   seeds   Whitney

6. The cotton gin made removing ______________________ from cotton easier.

7. ______________________ grew well in the South and was the most important crop.

8. Eli ______________________ invented the cotton gin.

C. Look up *compromise* in your glossary on page 292. Read the definition. Fill in the blanks.

9. compromise: an idea that is not exactly what either side wants but is good enough

for ______________________________________

10. Roger Sherman came up with a ______________________ about slavery that
was good enough for both the Northern states and the Southern states to like.

The Missouri Compromise

Name_______________________________

A. Fill in the puzzle using the word bank.

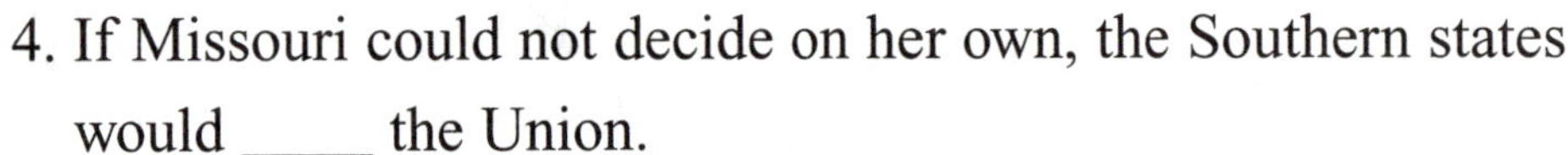

1. A compromise tries to make both _____ happy.

2. Henry _____ presented the Missouri Compromise to Congress.

3. The Missouri Territory wanted to become a _____.

4. If Missouri could not decide on her own, the Southern states would _____ the Union.

5. _____ was admitted to the Union as a *free* state.

6. _____ was admitted to the Union as a *slave* state.

7. The people of a _____ could not choose their own laws.

Henry Clay kept the United States together with the Missouri Compromise.

B. Use the boxed letters in Part A to complete the sentence.

8. The states were arguing about ____ ____ ____ ____ ____ ____ ____.

Santa Anna and his army killed the brave Texans at the Alamo. Among the men that died was Davy Crockett, a pioneer who wanted Texas to be free of Mexican rule. The Texan army honored these men by shouting **"Remember the Alamo!"** in the next battle. **Sam Houston**, leading the Texans, captured Santa Anna and led Texas to victory.

In the blank write *A* for Americans, *M* for Mexican, or *T* for Texans.

_______ 1. The Mexican leader said it was all right for _____ to move into Texas.

_______ 2. The _____ army was sent to Texas to make sure the Texans obeyed the laws.

_______ 3. The _____ president was Antonio López de Santa Anna.

_______ 4. After a few battles with Mexico, _____ thought that they had won their freedom.

_______ 5. Santa Anna and his army did not give up after their defeat by the _____.

_______ 6. Santa Anna led the _____ army against the Texans at the Alamo.

_______ 7. None of the fighting _____ survived the attack on the Alamo.

_______ 8. Sam Houston led the _____, shouting, "Remember the Alamo!"

_______ 9. Sam Houston captured Santa Anna, freeing Texas from _____ control.

_______10. Some _____ thought that making Texas a state might cause a war with Mexico.

Santa Anna surrenders to Sam Houston, leader of the Texas army.

Name________________________________

A. Fill in the blanks using the word banks.

cotton gin   farmland   Southern   territory

____

1. Eli Whitney invented the _____.

____

2. People in the Southern states bought more _____ and slaves because of the invention of the cotton gin.

____

3. Cotton was an important crop in the _____ states.

____

4. People who lived in a _____ could not vote for president.

free   Maine   Missouri   slaves

____

5. The question for new states was "Will this be a _____ or a slave state?"

____

6. In a free state, _____ were not allowed.

____

7. Henry Clay came up with the _____ Compromise.

____

8. The compromise let Missouri be a slave state and _____ be a free state.

B. Number the statements in the order in which they happened.

_______ Santa Anna sends his army to make sure the Texans obey Mexico's laws.

_______ The Texans form an army under the leadership of Sam Houston.

_______ Mexico allows Americans to move into Texas.

C. Number the statements in the order in which they happened.

_______ The Texans capture Santa Anna; the war between Mexico and the Texans ends.

_______ The Mexican army attacks the Texans at the Alamo.

_______ Texans want to make their land part of the United States.

The Alamo

Cause and Effect

Name_______________________

Match each *cause* in the first column with its *effect* in the second column by drawing a line from the cause to the effect.

Cause (Why) → **Effect (What Happened)**

Cause (Why)	Effect (What Happened)
1. Because President Polk did not want war with Mexico, he . . .	. . . were called property.
2. Because the number of free states was equal to the number of slave states in 1850, the North and the South . . .	. . . argued over whether California should be a slave or a free state.
3. Because slaves were not thought of as people, they . . .	. . . sent an ambassador to try to make peace.
4. Because the United States won the war with Mexico, the country . . .	. . . made another compromise.
5. Because Henry Clay did not want the country to split apart, he . . .	. . . gained land that stretched to the Pacific Ocean.
6. Because some Northerners thought owning a human being was wrong, they . . .	. . . wanted to abolish or get rid of slavery.

Because many people were against slavery, they helped runaway slaves get to free states.

*Cause **is the reason for an action. Effect is the result. For example: Because a person feels sorry for his sin, he turns to God for forgiveness.*** **(Bible principle from 2 Corinthians 7:10)**

People, Places, and Things

Name__________________________

A person, a place, and a thing are missing from each sentence. Choose a row to fill in the blanks. Place the words in the correct order.

People	Places	Things
men	Kansas	Bleeding Kansas
Harriet Beecher Stowe	South	Uncle Tom's Cabin
Harriet Tubman	Pennsylvania	slavery
Moses	North	Underground Railroad
people	Nebraska	compromise

1. ___________________________ escaped out of
   (person)

   ___________________ to the free state of ___________________ .
   (thing)   (place)

2. She was called ___________________ when she led slaves to the ___________________
   (person)   (place)

   on the ___________________ .
   (thing)

3. ___________________________ wrote
   (person)

   ___________________ about slavery in the ___________________ .
   (thing)   (place)

4. Congress made a ___________________ called the Kansas-
   (thing)

   ___________________ Act so ___________________ in all the territories
   (place)   (person)

   could choose for or against slavery.

5. ___________________ in ___________________ fought so much that the
   (person)   (place)

   territory was called ___________________ .
                          (thing)

Abraham Lincoln

Name_______________________

Write **T** if the statement is true and **F** if it is false.
Make each false statement true by correcting the underlined word(s).
Write the correct answer in the blank.

_______ 1. Abraham Lincoln was born into a <u>rich</u> family. _______________

_______ 2. Lincoln <u>read</u> books over and over. _______________

_______ 3. Lincoln was a <u>dependable</u> worker. _______________

_______ 4. Lincoln's nickname was "<u>Honest Lincoln</u>." _______________

_______ 5. While in Springfield, Lincoln became a famous <u>doctor</u>. _______________

_______ 6. Abraham Lincoln was <u>against</u> slavery. _______________

_______ 7. <u>Lincoln</u> said, "He who would be no slave must consent to have no slave." _______________

_______ 8. Lincoln said, "Those who deny <u>slavery</u> to others deserve it not for

themselves." _______________

_______ 9. Lincoln was a member of the <u>Democratic</u> party. _______________

______ 10. Lincoln ran for president of the United States in <u>1860</u>. _______________

Southerners and Slaves

Name_____________________

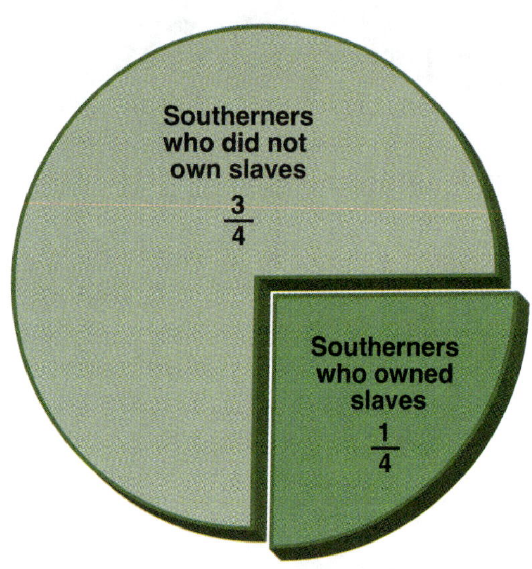

____

Harriet Tubman escaped from plantation owner Edward Brodas.

Read the *Learning How* steps on text page 146. Answer the questions.

1. Read the information on the circle graph. Read the possible titles for the graph. Choose the better title and write it on the line under the graph.
   A. Southerners and Northerners   B. Southerners and Slaves

2. What are the two parts shown inside the graph? _______________________

   A. Southerners who ____

   B. Southerners who ____

3. What part of Southerners owned slaves? _______________________________

4. What part of Southerners did not own slaves? _________________________

5. Which part is bigger?

   Southerners who ____

6. According to this graph, did most Southerners own slaves? _____________

North and South

Name______________________________

A. Put an *X* in the column to tell how the people in the North and the South were different.

		North	South
1. Where did most people live and work?	in cities		
	on farms or plantations		
2. How should the question about owning slaves be decided?	The United States should decide for all states.		
	Each state should decide for that state.		
3. How did each group react to problems between the North and South?	stayed in the Union		
	left the Union		

B. Fill in the blanks.

4. Abraham Lincoln was elected ____________________.

5. The Southern states left the ____________________.

6. The Southern states formed a ____________________ country.

7. The new country was called the ____________________ States of America.

8. The war began when the Southern states fired a shot on Fort ____________________.

The United States' rights are written in the Constitution. The rights that are not written in the Constitution are called **states' rights**. Some rights a state could decide for itself. The Southern states believed strongly in **states' rights**.

Name________________________________

A. Number the statements in the order in which they happened.

_______ 1. Americans move into Mexican land known as the Texas territory. (134)

_______ 2. Mexican soldiers try to make the Texans obey Mexican law. (134)

_______ 3. The war between the United States and Mexico begins. (137)

_______ 4. Texas becomes a state. (137)

_______ 5. The Texans capture Santa Anna and win freedom for Texas. (136)

B. Fill in the blanks using the word banks.

> cotton gin   free   Lincoln   property   slavery

6. Southerners bought more farmland and slaves after Eli Whitney's invention of the

___________________________ . (131)

7. Slaves were not thought of as people but were called ___________________ . (139)

8. To become a state, a territory had to decide to be slave or ______________ . (132)

9. ___________________ was not allowed in a free state. (138–39)

10. ___________________ said, "He who would be no slave must consent to have no slave." (145)

> Confederacy   Fort Sumter   Missouri   Southern   Union

11. After Lincoln became president, the South left the ______________ . (147)

12. When the South left the Union, it became the ______________ . (147)

13. Even before the ______________ Compromise, Southern states wanted to leave the Union. (133)

14. The ______________ states depended on cotton as an important crop. (131)

15. The Southern soldiers shot at the Union soldiers at ______________ . (148)

Stephen Foster's Songs

Name_______________________

Read the *Learning How* steps on text page 153.
Read the line graph to answer the questions.

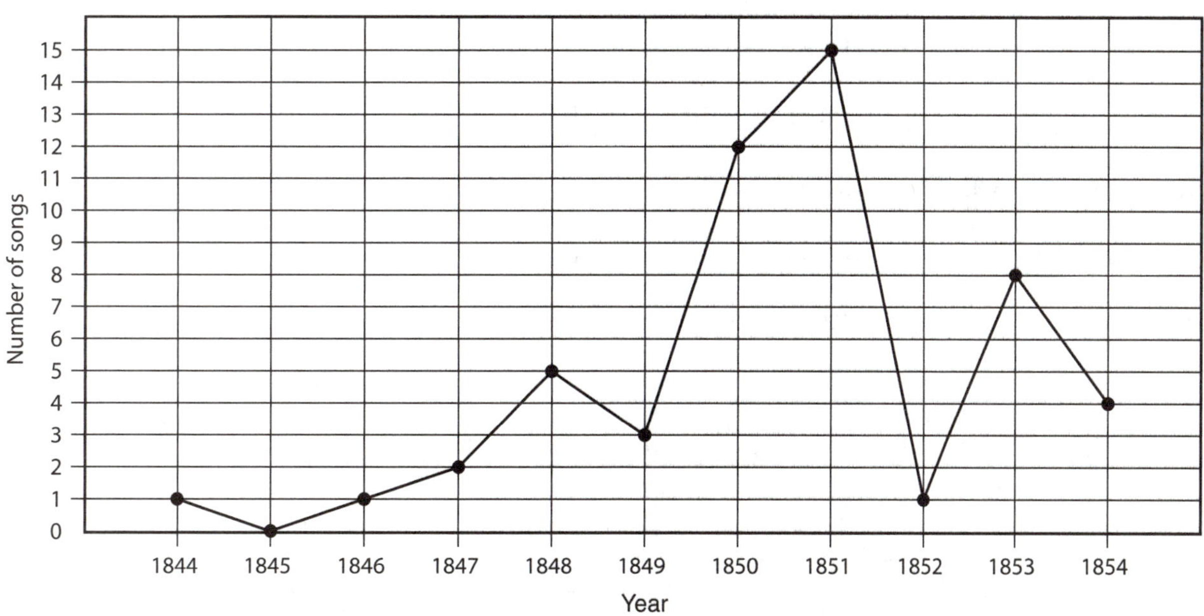

1. In which year did Stephen Foster publish his first song? _______________

2. In which year did he publish the most songs? _______________

   How many songs did he publish that year? _______________

3. In which year do we see no record of songs published?

   ____

4. Stephen Foster wrote "Oh, Susanna" in 1848.
   How many other songs did he write that year?

   ____

Stephen Foster

Songs

Name______________________________

A. Read the clues and fill in the puzzle.

1. the first American to make his living by writing songs

2. a type of song that people love to hear and sing

3. a Foster song written in 1848

4. where men started searching for gold in 1849

5. what Susanna was "a-walking down"

6. the color of the rose Susanna had in her hand

7. the place I come from "with my banjo on my knee"

B. Use the circled boxes in Part A to answer the question.

8. Which state has as its state song Foster's "Old Folks at Home"?

Heritage Studies 3
Worktext—Chapter 8

Musical Instruments

Name________________________

A. Look up the Bible references.
   Match the Bible verses with the musical instruments by writing the letter(s) in the blank. Answers may be used more than once.

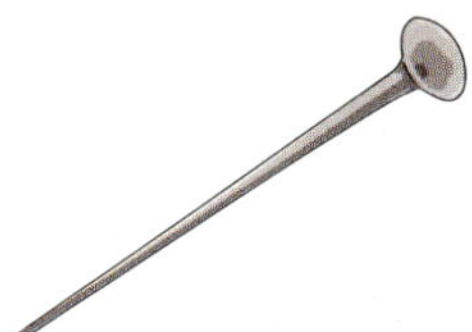

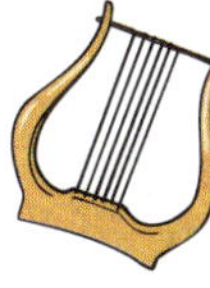

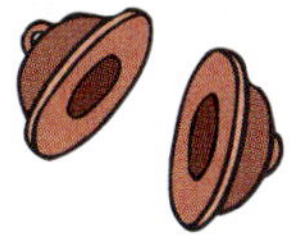

A. trumpet   B. harp or lyre   C. timbrel or tambourine   D. cymbals

_________________ 1. In Exodus 15:20 Miriam played this instrument.

_________________ 2. In Ezra 3:10 the priests and Levites used these instruments to praise God.

_________________ 3. Psalm 98:5 instructs us to sing to the Lord with this instrument.

_________________ 4. In 1 Chronicles 13:8 all Israel sang and played before God.

B. Draw a line to match the picture with the way that the instrument is played.

blowing

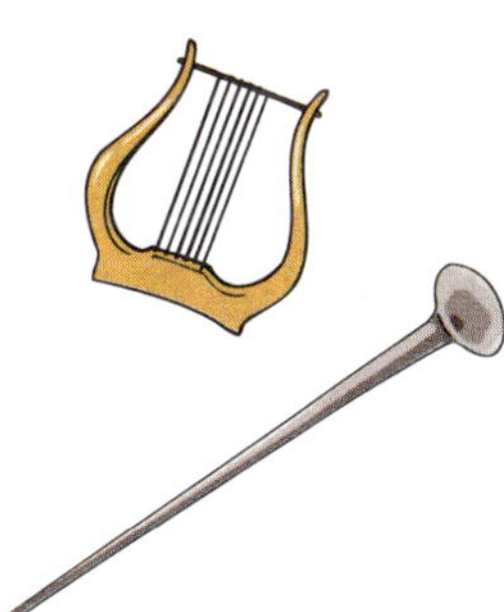

tapping or hitting

plucking

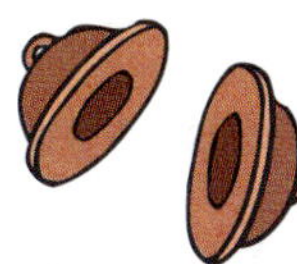

5. How are all of these musical instruments used in the Bible?

____

____

Study Questions

A. Fill in the blanks using the word bank.

> blowing   dogies   folksongs   Foster   glory   popular

1. Songs that people love to hear and sing are called _________________ songs.

2. The songwriter Stephen _________________ wrote "Oh, Susanna!" and was the first American to make his living by writing songs.

3. Cowboys sang songs to their little _________________ or stray calves.

4. We do not know who wrote the words and music to _________________.

5. Musical instruments can be played by _________________ into them, tapping or hitting them, or plucking the strings.

6. David used his harp to bring _________________ to God.

God wants us to praise Him with music.
(Bible principle from Psalm 150:3–5)

B. Match the song lines to the song title by writing the letter in the blank.

> A. "Oh, Susanna!"   B. "Git Along, Little Dogies"

_______ 7. I come from Alabama with my banjo on my knee;
I'm going to Lou'siana, my true love for to see.

_______ 8. As I was a-walkin' one mornin' for pleasure,
I spied a cowpuncher come ridin' along.

_______ 9. Whoopee ti yi yo, git along, little dogies;
You know that Montana will be your new home.

Dogies were calves that got separated from their mothers on the range. Cowboys would find the calves and bring them back into the herd.

Union and Confederate Bugles

Name_______________________

Read the information about bugles. Answer the questions.

The sounds of the guns and cannons going off were loud. A soldier could not hear or talk to the man next to him. So the armies began to use musicians. A bugle could make the commander's orders louder. The early bugle was made of brass or copper. It was similar to a trumpet but had no valves.

Buglers were often young boys. They had to learn many calls. About twenty-five general calls were like a clock. They let the men know when to rise, eat, and meet. There were about twenty-four battle calls. A bugler passed along the calls from other buglers. He could spy on the enemy by listening to their calls. It was hard for a soldier to know which bugle call was for him. In some battles some of the soldiers would move back while others would charge.

1. What was the problem with a commander yelling his orders?

   ____

   ____

2. What instrument is the bugle similar to? _______________________

   ____

   How is a bugle different from this instrument? _______________

   ____

3. Who were often the buglers? _______________________________

4. How were bugles used?

   ____

   • for general calls like a _______________________

   • for calls during a _______________________

     ____

   • to _______________________ along other bugle calls

     ____

   • to _______________________ on enemy soldiers

5. What problem did the soldiers have with the bugle calls?

   ____

Study Questions

A. Fill in the blanks using the word bank.

> Emmett   Howe   Mason   national   spirituals

1. Slave songs or ____________________ tell about the slaves' faith in God to protect and deliver them. (157)

2. Lowell ____________________ wrote over one thousand hymns. (159)

3. Dan ____________________ was the Northerner, loyal to the Union, who wrote "Dixie." (160)

4. Julia Ward ____________________ wrote the words to "The Battle Hymn of the Republic." (163)

5. ____________________ songs are part of America's heritage. (163)

B. Write the letter that matches the song title to the songwriter or the type of song.

> A. spiritual   C. Lowell Mason
> B. war song for the South   D. war song for the North

______ 6. "Dixie" (160)

______ 7. "Go Down, Moses" (157–58)

______ 8. "The Battle Hymn of the Republic" (163–64)

______ 9. "There Is a Fountain" (159)

C. Write the letter that matches the song lines to the correct song title.

> A. "Go Down, Moses"   B. "Dixie"   C. "The Battle Hymn of the Republic"

______ 10. I wish I was in the land of cotton,
Old times there are not forgotten. (161)

______ 11. "Let my people go.
If not, I'll strike your first-born dead!" (158)

______ 12. O be swift, my soul, to answer Him! Be jubilant, my feet!
Our God is marching on. (164)

Chapter Review

Name_______________________________

A. Draw a line from the songwriter to the song he or she wrote.

1. Dan Emmett "The Battle Hymn of the Republic" (163–64)

2. Stephen Foster "Dixie" (160–61)

3. Julia Ward Howe "Oh, Susanna" (151–52)

4. Lowell Mason "Nearer, My God, to Thee" (159)

B. Match the song lines to the song title by writing the letter in the blank.

A. "Oh, Susanna!" D. "Go Down, Moses"

B. "Git Along, Little Dogies" E. "The Battle Hymn of the Republic"

C. "Dixie"

______ 5. I come from Alabama with my banjo on my knee;
I'm going to Lou'siana, my true love for to see. (152)

______ 6. As I was a-walkin' one mornin' for pleasure,
I spied a cowpuncher come ridin' along. (155)

______ 7. Way down in Egypt land,
Tell ol' Pharaoh to let my people go! (158)

______ 8. Whoopee ti yi yo, git along, little dogies;
You know that Montana will be your new home. (155)

______ 9. A red, red rose was in her hand,
A tear was in her eye;
I said, "I come from Alabam'." (152)

______ 10. I wish I was in the land of cotton,
Old times there are not forgotten. (161)

______ 11. "Let my people go.
If not, I'll strike your first-born dead!" (158)

______ 12. Glory, glory, hallelujah!
His truth is marching on. (164)

Name______________________

Lowell Mason loved music as a young boy. God gave him musical talents, and he used them to please the Lord. Mason learned how to lead a choir, and he taught himself to play many instruments. He wrote the notes or music part of a hymn. He felt that teaching music to children was important, so he became one of the first school teachers to teach music. When you listen to a hymn by Lowell Mason, remember that he wrote the tune and someone else wrote the words. What talent has God given you? Will you use it for Him?

C. Write *T* if the statement is true and *F* if it is false.
Make each false statement true by correcting the underlined word(s).
Write the correct answer in the blank.

_______ 13. We do not know who wrote most early <u>folksongs</u>. (154) _______________

_______ 14. Little <u>horn</u> is another name for longhorn calves. (154) _______________

_______ 15. <u>Spirituals</u> told about the slaves' faith in God. (157) _______________

_______ 16. "Dixie," written by a Northerner, was a favorite <u>Confederate</u> war song. (160)

_______ 17. <u>Julia Ward Howe</u> wrote "The Battle Hymn of the Republic" to the tune of

"John Brown's Body." (163–64) _______________

_______ 18. The Northern war song was "<u>Hail to the Victors</u>." (163–64)

_______ 19. Stephen Foster made his living by writing <u>songs</u>. (151) _______________

_______ 20. Lowell Mason wrote over <u>one million</u>

hymns. (159) _______________

"Whether therefore ye eat, or drink, or whatsoever ye do, do all to the glory of God."
(1 Corinthians 10:31)

Union and Confederacy   Name_________________________

A. Write *T* if the statement is true and *F* if it is false. Make each false statement true by correcting the underlined word(s). Write the correct answer in the blank. Read the Think About It below.

_______ 1. The firing at Fort <u>Sumter</u> did not kill one soldier. __________

_______ 2. <u>Charleston</u>, South Carolina, was not damaged during the firing on Fort

Sumter. _______________________

_______ 3. Lincoln called for volunteers to fight for the <u>South</u>. __________

_______ 4. <u>Abraham Lincoln</u> was president of the Confederate States of America.

_______ 5. In 1861 the Confederate States of America had <u>eleven</u> states. __________

_______ 6. The <u>Union</u> capital was Richmond, Virginia. __________

_______ 7. <u>Journals</u> tell us much about the American Civil War. __________

_______ 8. The <u>capital</u> of a country is where leaders make laws. __________

B. Who had the advantage, the Union or the Confederacy? Put a check mark under the correct column.

	Union	Confederacy
9. More factories		
10. More railroads		
11. More free people and firearms		
12. Best military leaders		
13. Needed fewer men to protect homeland		

When the states in the South left the United States, they needed a new president. **Jefferson Davis** was elected president of the Confederate States of America. Richmond, Virginia, became the capital and Davis's new home.

The First Big Battle: Manassas (Bull Run)

Name_______________________

A. Fill in the blanks using the word banks.

> practice   Union   volunteers   Washington, DC

1. To *drill* means to _______________________.

2. _______________________ were men who had offered to fight for their country.

3. General McDowell, a _______________________ officer, led the battle at Bull Run.

4. The Union army wanted to capture Manassas Junction to protect its capital, _______________________.

> Bull Run   Confederate   slaves   soldiers

5. The Battle of _______________________ was the first big battle of the Civil War.

6. General Jackson was a _______________________ officer.

7. Stonewall Jackson started a Sunday school for _______________________.

8. Stonewall Jackson was accidentally shot by one of his own _______________________.

After the Battle of Bull Run, Thomas J. Jackson was nicknamed Stonewall Jackson.

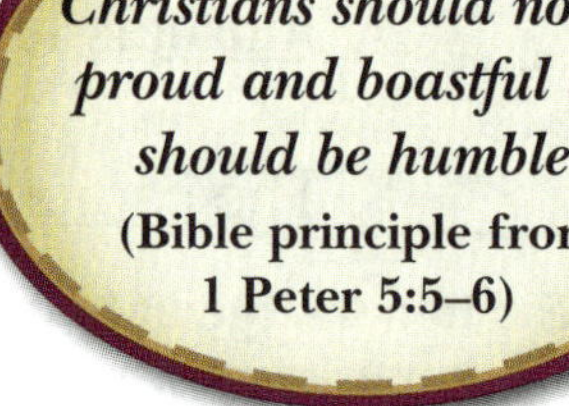

B. Answer the questions in a complete sentence.

9. Why was Thomas Jackson called Stonewall Jackson?

10. What is one reason Stonewall Jackson is considered a hero?

Study Questions

Name____________________________

A. Complete the chart.

	North	South
1. Another name	Union	
2. Capital	Washington, DC	
3. President		Jefferson Davis
4. Uniform color		gray
5. General	George McClellan	
6. Nickname		Rebels

B. Fill in the blanks using the word bank.

balloon   Robert E. Lee   George McClellan   North

7. President Lincoln chose ________________________ to be the new general of the Union army because he was a great planner.

8. Women sent their best silk ball gowns to make a ________________________ to spy on the enemy.

9. The new leader of the Confederate army was ________________________.

10. General Lee marched the Confederate army into the ________________________ toward Pennsylvania.

President Lincoln meets with General George McClellan and other Union soldiers.

Letter to Home

Name_______________________

Pretend that you are a Confederate or Union soldier writing a letter to your family back home. You may want to write about your uniform, a battle, or your leader.

Complete the crossword puzzle.

Across

3. "freeing"

7. groups of soldiers

8. became nurses during the Civil War

Down

1. famous Civil War photographer

2. worst single day's battle

4. property taken from the enemy

5. someone who wanted to do away with slavery

6. first black Union officer

abolitionist
Antietam
Brady
contraband
Delany
emancipation
regiments
women

Some people wanted to abolish slavery in America. **Abolish** means "to do away with." Someone who wanted to do away with slavery was called an **abolitionist**. **Frederick Douglass** was a famous abolitionist.

North Wind Picture Archives

Study Questions

Name______________________________

A. Write *T* if the statement is true and *F* if it is false. Make each false statement true by correcting the underlined word. Write the correct answer in the blank.

_______ 1. <u>More</u> soldiers were killed at Gettysburg than at any other

Civil War battle. _______________

_______ 2. The Battle of Gettysburg was the turning point of the

<u>Revolutionary</u> War. _______________

_______ 3. President <u>Davis</u> chose Ulysses S. Grant to be the Union

general. _______________

_______ 4. Both sides were glad when the long war ended after <u>two</u>

years. _______________

Robert E. Lee

Ulysses S. Grant

B. Fill in the blanks using the word bank.

| amend | Appomattox | Booth | Thirteenth |

5. Lee was the Confederate general that surrendered at _______________
Court House.

6. In order to emancipate the slaves, the United States had to _______________,
or change, the Constitution.

7. The _______________ Amendment freed the slaves in the United States.

8. John Wilkes _______________, a Southerner, shot President Lincoln.

Amend means "to change for the better." To make changes in our government, we amend the Constitution. The Thirteenth **Amendment** changed the Constitution. It ended slavery in the United States forever. Slaves were emancipated.

Chapter Review

Name________________________

A. Write the name of the person to whom the statement applies.

Lincoln   Grant   Lee   Jackson

1. He said that it was "only a question of time" until the Thirteenth Amendment would pass. (189)

2. His troops were tired and supplies were low; he surrendered at Appomattox Court House. (187)

3. He was shot by John Wilkes Booth, a Southerner, days after the war ended. (190)

4. His nickname was "Stonewall." (172)

5. He allowed Southern troops to keep their horses. (188)

6. He was accidentally shot by one of his own men. (172)

7. He became leader of the Union army after winning battles in the West. (186)

8. He took charge of the Grays and was the best Confederate general. (176)

9. He announced the Emancipation Proclamation. (179)

10. His men loved him even though he had to surrender. (188)

11. He ordered that food be sent to the Southern army. (188)

Name_______________________________

B. Match the term with the definition by writing the term from the word bank in the blank.

12. to free (179) _______________________________

13. to do away with (177, 139) _______________________________

14. to change for the better (189) _______________________________

abolish

amend

emancipate

C. Complete the chart using the word bank.

| blue | Grant | Lee | men, factories | Richmond, VA |
| Davis | gray | Lincoln | military leaders | Washington, DC |

	Union	**Confederacy**
15. Capital (168)		
16. President (166)		
17. General (187)		
18. Uniform color (173)		
19. Advantage (166–67)		

D. Fill in the blanks using the word bank.

| Bull Run | Emancipation | Gettysburg | slaves |

20. The Thirteenth Amendment freed the _______________________________ in the United States. (189)

21. The first major battle of the Civil War was at _______________________________. (170–71)

22. The _______________________________ Proclamation freed the slaves in the South. (179)

23. _______________________________ was the major turning point of the Civil War. (182, 185)

Celebrations

Name_______________________

**A. If the statement is true, write _T_.
If the statement is false, write _F_.**

_______ 1. George Washington was born in 1732.

_______ 2. Washington was greatly loved and admired by his countrymen.

_______ 3. Abraham Lincoln is called the Father of Our Country.

_______ 4. Lincoln came from a poor family.

_______ 5. Lincoln led the United States during the War for Independence.

_______ 6. Lincoln and Washington were both born in February.

_______ 7. Lincoln and Washington have the same birthday.

_______ 8. The Washington Monument is in New York Harbor.

_______ 9. Americans celebrate Lincoln's and Washington's birthdays on the same day.

_______ 10. The third Monday in February is Presidents' Day.

_______ 11. Monuments are also called _memorials_.

_______ 12. The Lincoln Memorial and the Washington Monument are in Washington, DC.

B. Circle all the numbers in Part A that are true. Using only the circled numbers, connect the dots to draw a picture of a monument.

13. The famous monument is the _______________________.

Name________________________________

EASTER

by Eileen Berry

Early in the morning
At the dawning of the day,
Softly come the women
To the tomb where Jesus lay.
Empty now they find it:
"**R**isen," hear the angels say!

**Use the letters in *Easter* to make your own poem or acrostic.
An example is given. You may use the word bank or think of other words about Easter.**

Easter Word Bank:	**Easter Morn**
E Easter, Earthquake, Empty	**E**arly,
A Angels, Away, Appeared, Afraid, Amazed, Arose	**A**ngels
S Sepulcher, Stone, Savior, Spices, Sacrifice, Sins, Son of God	**S**at
T Tomb, Tell, Third day	**T**elling,
E Early morning, Eternal, Everlasting, Empty tomb	"**E**ver
R Risen, Resurrection, Rolled away, Remember, Redeemer	**R**isen."

E
A
S
T
E
R

Holidays

A. If the statement is true of Easter, write *Easter* in the blank.
If the statement is not true of Easter, write *false.*

_______________ 1. On Easter we remember that Jesus died on the cross.

_______________ 2. On Easter we remember that Jesus rose from the dead.

_______________ 3. On Easter we think of people who died in wars.

_______________ 4. On Easter we celebrate by watching a fireworks display.

_______________ 5. On Easter we remember that we can live forever with Jesus in heaven.

"How that Christ died for our sins according to the scriptures; And that he was buried, and that he rose again the third day according to the scriptures."
1 Corinthians 15:3–4

B. If the statement is true of Memorial Day, write *Memorial* in the blank.
If the statement is not true of Memorial Day, write *false.*

_______________ 6. On Memorial Day we celebrate America's birthday.

_______________ 7. On Memorial Day we think of people who died in wars.

_______________ 8. On Memorial Day we give gifts to our friends.

_______________ 9. On Memorial Day flowers and flags remind us that people gave their lives to make America free.

_______________ 10. Memorial Day was first celebrated after the Civil War.

On Memorial Day flags are placed on the graves of soldiers who gave their lives for America.

Complete the crossword puzzle using the word bank (text pages 198–200 and 269–71).

colonies	liberty
eagle	loyalty
fireworks	red
fly	rules
July	seal
June	states

Across

2. The color blue on the flag stands for _____.

4. On the Fourth of July, we might watch _____.

6. The national bird is an _____.

7. Americans celebrate Independence Day in the month of _____.

8. The sign that appears on all important papers of the United States government is the Great _____.

9. The colonists were unhappy with King George's _____.

Down

1. On Flag Day, Americans should _____ the flag.

2. The color white on the flag stands for _____.

3. The thirteen stripes on the flag stand for the thirteen _____.

5. The fifty stars on the flag stand for the fifty _____.

7. Americans celebrate Flag Day in the month of _____.

9. The color on the flag that stands for courage is _____.

Study Questions

A. Fill in the blanks using the word bank.

> Civil   February   Independence   Lincoln   monument   Washington

1. George Washington and Abraham Lincoln were both born in

   _______________________ .

2. The Father of Our Country is George _______________________ .

3. George Washington led the American army during the War for

   _______________________ .

4. Abraham Lincoln was a brave, wise leader during the _______________________ War.

5. A building or statue in memory of a person is called a _______________________ .

6. The Washington Monument and the _______________________ Memorial are in Washington, DC.

B. Draw a line to match the holiday with what it celebrates.

7. Presidents' Day   A. the risen Jesus Christ

8. Easter   B. those who have died in America's wars

9. Memorial Day   C. birthdays of Washington and Lincoln

10. Flag Day   D. the freedom of Americans

11. Independence Day   E. the American flag's "birthday"

C. Draw a line to match the color on the flag with its meaning.

12. red   A. loyalty

13. white   B. courage

14. blue   C. liberty and freedom

Letter of Thankfulness

Name___________________________

Write a letter of thankfulness to Columbus or to a Pilgrim.

Heritage Studies 3
Worktext—Chapter 10

Chapter Review

Name_______________________________

A. Complete the chart about the holidays you have studied.

Holiday	Month Celebrated	What We Remember
1. Presidents' Day		Washington's and Lincoln's birthdays (194)
2.	March or April	Christ's Resurrection (196, 206)
3. Memorial Day		people who have died in America's wars (197)
4.		the United States flag (198)
5. Independence Day		America's freedom (200)
6.		Columbus's finding "new" land (202)
7. Thanksgiving		thanking God (204, 277)
8.		Christ's birth (205)

B. Name the color from the American flag that represents each term. (198)

9. Courage – _______________

10. Liberty and freedom – _______________

11. Loyalty – _______________

Name________________________

C. Fill in the blanks using the word banks.

| Civil | Columbus | Father | Fourth of July | Washington, DC |

12. The ________________ of Our Country is George Washington. (193)

13. The Washington Monument and the Lincoln Memorial are located in

________________. (195)

14. Abraham Lincoln led America through the ________________ War. (194)

15. Independence Day is also called the ________________. (200)

16. Christopher ________________ believed that the earth was shaped like
a ball. (202)

| Asia | God | Indians | Jesus | Pilgrims |

17. Columbus sailed west from Spain trying to find

an easier way to ________________. (202)

18. Columbus called the island people

________________. (203)

19. Those present at the first Thanksgiving were the

Separatists, other ________________, and

Indians. (204)

20. We do not know the exact date on which ________________ was born. (205)

21. When we celebrate holidays, we need to be reminded of the things

________________ has given us. (206)

*We should remember
God's great love and
goodness toward us and
praise His name.*
**(Bible principle from
Psalm 107:8)**

Early Travel

Complete the crossword puzzle using the word bank.

boat	car	horse	wagons
canals	dirt	locomotive	walking

Across

3. Boats traveled on rivers, oceans, streams, and ____.

6. A huge, shiny black monster puffing smoke was a ____.

7. The roads during the early years of travel were made of ____.

8. Sometimes horses pulled ____ to carry goods.

Down

1. One section of a train is called a ____.

2. If you travel by using your feet, you are ____.

4. A vehicle for traveling on water is a ____.

5. An important farm animal to ride was a ____.

First Railroads

Name_______________________________

_______ 1. People in the early 1800s <u>liked</u> traveling. _______________

_______ 2. Wagon wheels rolled along on <u>wood</u> or iron rails. _______________

_______ 3. Steamboats could travel up a river <u>against</u> the current. _______________

_______ 4. Peter Cooper built the first successful <u>steamboat</u>. _______________

_______ 5. Most people did not believe that steam engines could pull <u>wagons</u> along the

railroads. _______________

Locomotives replaced the horse-drawn wagons.

_______ 6. A <u>locomotive</u> was a small steam engine

on wheels. _______________

_______ 7. Peter Cooper built the <u>Tom Thumb</u>, a steam engine that could travel over land.

____

_______ 8. The Tom Thumb ran on the <u>Washington</u> and Ohio Railroad.

____

_______ 9. The big locomotive built by Mathias Baldwin was called Old <u>Smoky</u>.

____

_______ 10. Working toy trains are called <u>model</u> trains. _______________

_______ 11. The Tom Thumb was much <u>smaller</u> than Old Ironsides. _______________

Different Jobs

Early steam locomotives had to stop for water and fuel. Wood was cut and left along the tracks for the fireman to fill the firebox. The train men and passengers hauled water from a nearby stream to the train. Imagine having to get off the train to carry water in a bucket!

Engineer

Fireman

A. Match the job descriptions by writing *E* for engineer and *F* for fireman in the correct column.

1. Shovels coal into the firebox

2. Watches the track ahead

3. Keeps the train moving at a good speed

4. Keeps the fire going

5. Is the boss on the train

6. Keeps the water level in the boiler just right

B. Fill in the blanks using the word bank.

> boiler   coal   steam   water

7. Water that is boiled in the boiler of the locomotive causes ________________.

8. If the fire in the ________________ gets too hot, the boiler might blow up.

9. The two kinds of fuel used in steam engines were ________________ and wood.

10. Steam locomotives had to stop along the track for more ________________ and more wood or coal.

Name_______________________

Song of the Train

by David McCord

Clickety-clack,
Wheels on the track,
This is the way
They begin the attack:
Click-ety-clack,
Click-ety-clack,
Click-ety-*clack*-ety,
Click-ety
Clack.

Clickety-clack,
Over the crack,
Faster and faster
The song of the track:
Clickety-clack,
Clickety-clack,
Clickety, clackety,
Clackety
Clack.

Riding in front,
Riding in back,
Everyone hears
The song of the track:
Clickety-clack,
Clickety-clack,
Clickety, *clickety*,
Clackety
Clack.

From *ONE AT A TIME* by David McCord. Copyright © 1965, 1966 by David McCord.
By permission of Little, Brown and Co., Inc.

Map Scales

Name______________________

1. Study the key. How many miles does one inch represent? ______________ miles

2. Using the map of the make-believe country and a ruler, fill in the chart.

Center Station to Southport	inch(es)	miles
Center Station to End-of-the-Track	inch(es)	miles
Whistlestop to By-the-Way	inch(es)	miles
Center Station to Clickety-Clack	inch(es)	miles

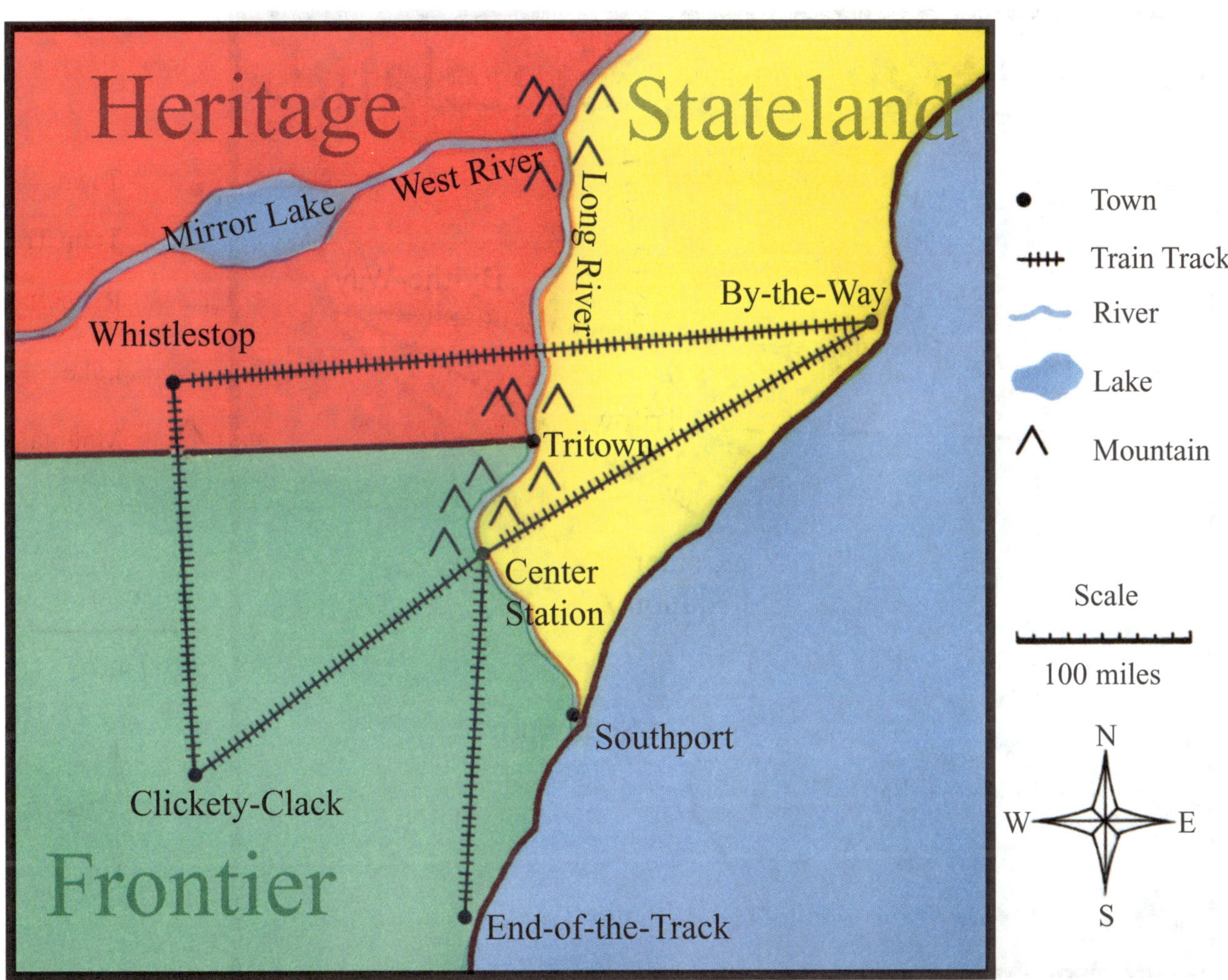

Map Skills

Name___________________________

Use the map of the make-believe country to answer the questions.

1. In what state is Mirror Lake?
   ○ Heritage   ○ Stateland

2. What river borders the states of Heritage and Stateland?
   ○ Long River   ○ West River

3. In what town do the three states meet?
   ○ Center Station   ○ Tritown

4. Which way is the shorter distance to travel from Whistlestop to Center Station?
   ○ by land   ○ by train

5. In what town could you use a boat for transportation?
   ○ Clickety-Clack   ○ Southport

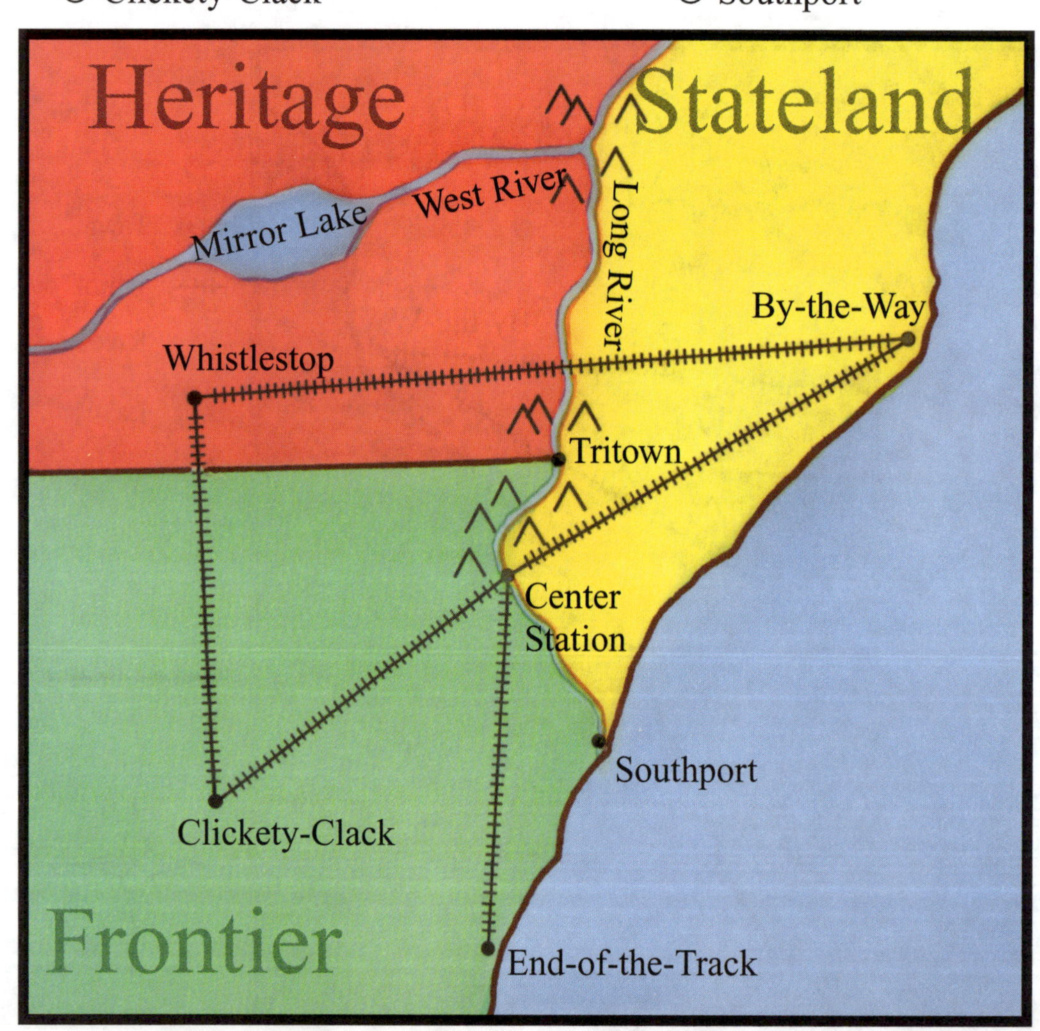

Transcontinental Railroad

Name_______________________________

Fill in the blanks using the word banks.

Omaha   Promontory   Sacramento

1. The Central Pacific Railroad began laying tracks in

_______________________________,

California.

2. The Union Pacific Railroad's tracks

began in _______________________________,

Nebraska.

3. The tracks of the two railroad companies met at _______________________________ Point, Utah.

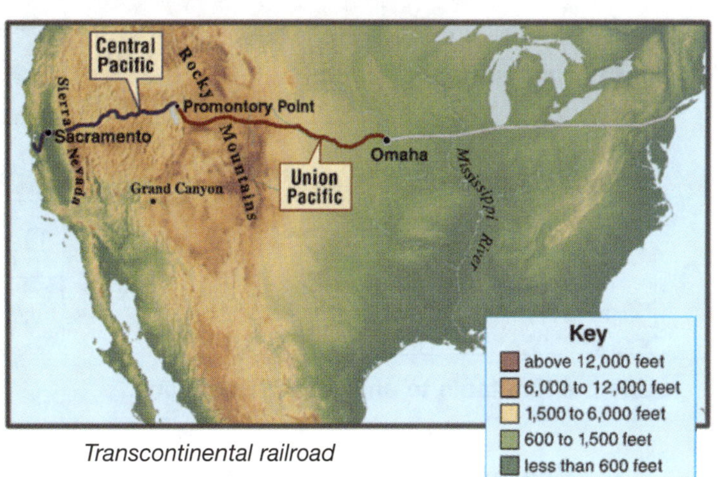

Transcontinental railroad

Central   Railroad   Union

4. The _______________________________ Act of 1862 gave two companies the right to build the first transcontinental railroad.

5. The _______________________________ Pacific Railroad worked faster on flat land.

6. The _______________________________ Pacific Railroad Company worked hard to dig tunnels and lay track through the mountains.

continent   Lincoln   transcontinental

7. President _______________________________ signed the Railroad Act of 1862.

8. The two railroad companies worked for almost eight years to complete the

_______________________________ railroad.

9. *Transcontinental* means "across the _______________________________."

Timetable

Name________________________

Train Name	Train Number	Days of Operation	Towns	Departure	Arrival
Thundercloud	18	Monday and Friday	Eagle Point to Downing	7:40 a.m.	9:40 a.m.
			Downing to White Plains	10:40 a.m.	1:40 p.m.
			White Plains to Junction	4:30 p.m.	8:30 p.m.

Use the timetable to answer the questions.

Railroad depot in Independence, Missouri

1. What is the name of the train? ________________________

2. What is the train's number? ________________________

3. On what two days of the week does the train operate or run?

________________________ and ________________________

4. What time does the train depart or leave from Eagle Point? ________________________

   What time does the train arrive at Downing? ________________________

   How long is the trip from Eagle Point to Downing? ________________________

5. What time does the train arrive at Downing? ________________________

   What time does it leave Downing? ________________________

   How long is the wait in Downing before the train departs for White Plains?

   ____

6. What time does Thundercloud leave White Plains? ________________________

   What time does it arrive at Junction? ________________________

   How long is the trip from White Plains to Junction? ________________________

Heritage Studies 3
Worktext—Chapter 11

Time Zones

Name______________________________

**Read the *Learning How* steps on text page 223.
Answer the questions using the map.**

1. Circle your state.

2. What color is your time zone on the map? _______________________

3. What time zone do you live in? _______________________

4. When it is 5:00 a.m. in Virginia, what time is it in California? _______________________

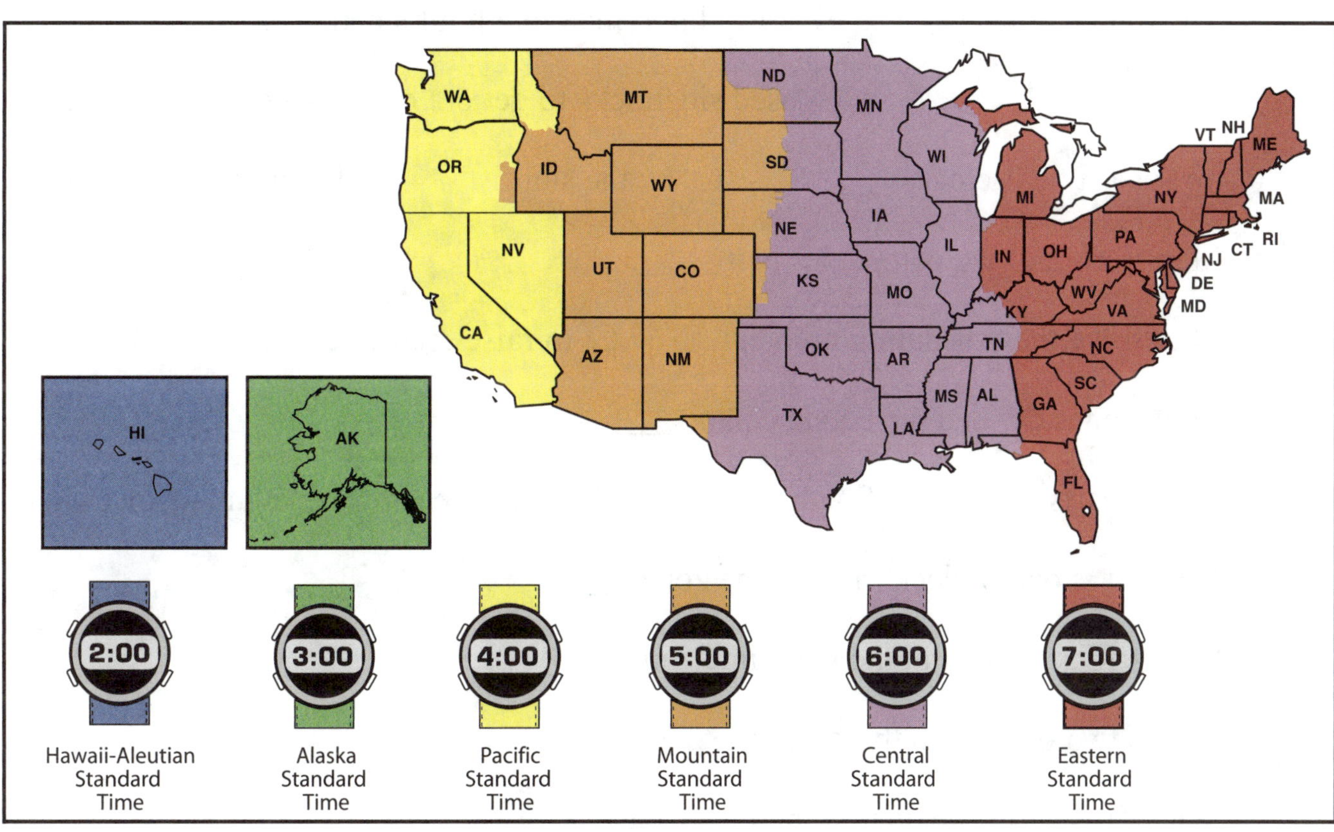

Study Questions

Fill in the circle.

1. George Westinghouse invented _____.

   ○ moving brake wheels that stopped the train

   ○ air brakes that used one switch to stop the train

2. The brakeman's job included _____.

   ○ running across all the cars and setting the brakes

   ○ tooting the whistle three times to stop the train

3. The train engineer _____. ○ was a hired man that built sidetracks

   ○ used sidetracks to get out of the way of another train

4. Towns set their clocks _____. ○ by the sun ○ by the train schedule

5. Men from railroad companies met _____.

   ○ to solve the scheduling problem ○ to raise their rates

6. Time zones divided the country into _____.

   ○ two parts, North and South ○ four parts, each part having its own time

7. When it is one o'clock in one time zone, _____.

   ○ it is four o'clock in the next time zone

   ○ it is two o'clock in the next time zone

8. When it is early evening on the East Coast, _____.

   ○ it is early evening on the West Coast ○ it is afternoon on the West Coast

9. Steam locomotives are _____. ○ found in museums and railroad yards today

   ○ a fast and convenient way to travel today

Chapter Review

Name_______________________________

A. Fill in the blanks using the word bank.

> Central   sidetracks   steamboat   two   Union

1. The Railroad Act of 1862 gave _________________ companies the right to build the first transcontinental railroad. (217)

   ____

2. The _________________ Pacific Railroad began laying tracks in Sacramento, California. (218)

3. The _________________ Pacific Railroad began laying tracks in Omaha, Nebraska. (218)

4. _________________ were built to keep trains from running into each other. (221)

5. The _________________ can travel up a river, against the current. (212)

B. Label the diagram using the word bank. (214)

> boiler   coal   fireman   locomotive   steam

6. _________________
   shovels coal into the firebox and keeps the fire burning

7. _________________
   fuel used to keep a steam engine going

8. _________________
   where fire causes the water to get boiling hot

9. _________________
   a steam engine on wheels

10. _________________
    what water turns into if kept in the boiler

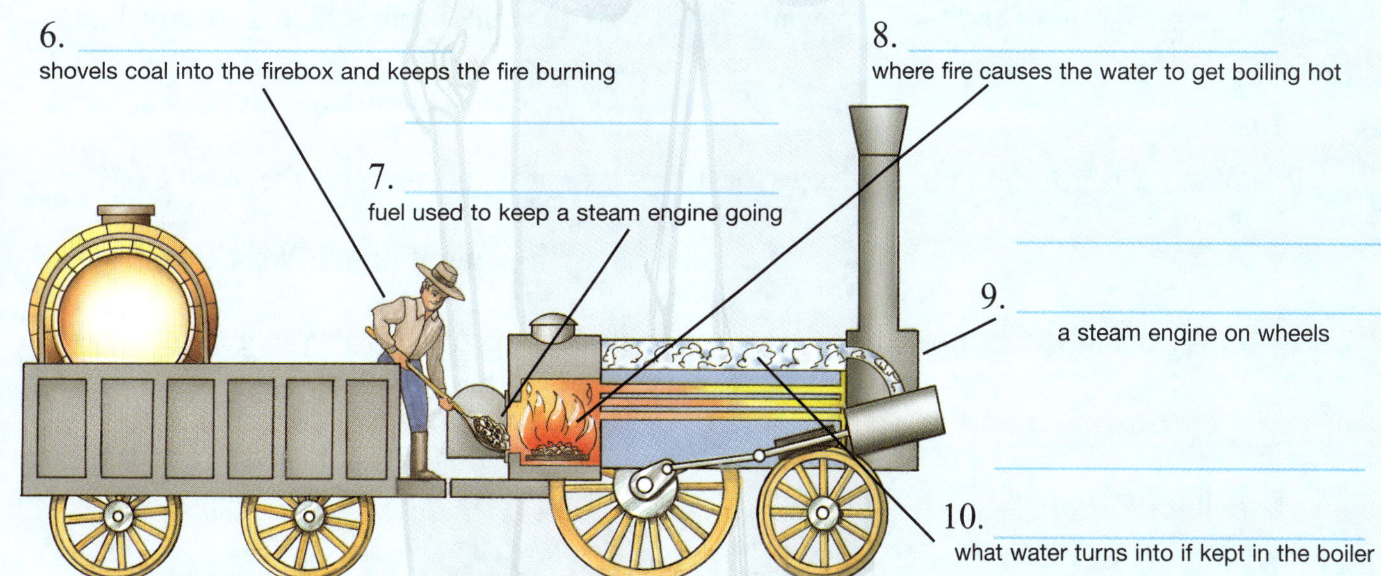

Early locomotive

Name_______________________________

C. Fill in the chart.

Who	What	Other Information
11.	Tom Thumb	built small steam engine (212)
12. Mathias Baldwin		full-sized train (213)
13. George Westinghouse		inventor (220)
14.	Railroad Act of 1862	helped the railroad (217)
15.	shovels coal	keeps fire going (215)
16. engineer		train boss (215)

D. Fill in the circle.

17. The size of the locomotive Old Ironsides ____. ○ was bigger than the Tom Thumb
(213)
    ○ was smaller than the Tom Thumb

18. The elevation of the Sierra Nevada ____. ○ is greater than Omaha, Nebraska
(219)
    ○ is less than Omaha, Nebraska

19. When it is afternoon in the East Coast, ____. ○ it is morning on the West Coast
    ○ it is night on the West Coast

20. Early steam locomotives had to ____. ○ stop frequently for passengers
    ○ stop often for more water and fuel

21. If the fire in the boiler of the train got too hot, ____. (215)
    ○ the train might move too slowly
    ○ the boiler might blow up

Will went out to saddle his horse. On his head he wore a felt **hat** to keep off the sun and rain. He sometimes used it to fan a fire and to carry water. Around his neck he wore a **bandanna**, which he used to protect his neck from the sun or to cover his nose and mouth from the blowing dust. Once he had used the bandanna as a bandage. He pulled on his **gauntlets**, which he needed to protect his hands from rope burns and blisters. His **chaps** would protect his legs from the brush and brambles on the cattle drive. The last of his clothing was his **boots**. The pointed toes slid into the stirrups, and the high heels kept his feet in place.

A. List the uses for each piece of clothing.

Hat—keeps off _______________ and _______________;

    fans a _______________;

    carries _______________

Bandanna—protects neck from _______________;

    keeps dust out of _______________ and

    _______________;

    used as a _______________

Gauntlets—protect _______________;

    prevent _______________ and

    ____

Chaps—protect legs from _______________ and _______________

Boots—slide into _______________; keep _______________ in stirrups

Name______________________________

Will whistled, and the big pinto horse with the dark mane and tail came forward. It wasn't really Will's horse. All the horses belonged to the owner of the Triple J Ranch. But this was the horse Will liked to ride the most. Pulling hard on the **cinch**, he tightened the saddle and secured the **ties**. The **skirt** of the saddle would protect him during his long ride. As he swung into the **seat**, his chaps swished against the leather **fender** of the saddle. His boots slid easily into the **stirrups**. Will adjusted the reins and then rested his hand on the **horn** of the saddle. With his bedroll placed against the **cantle**, Will was ready for the long ride.

B. Label the parts of this 1850s Texas saddle.

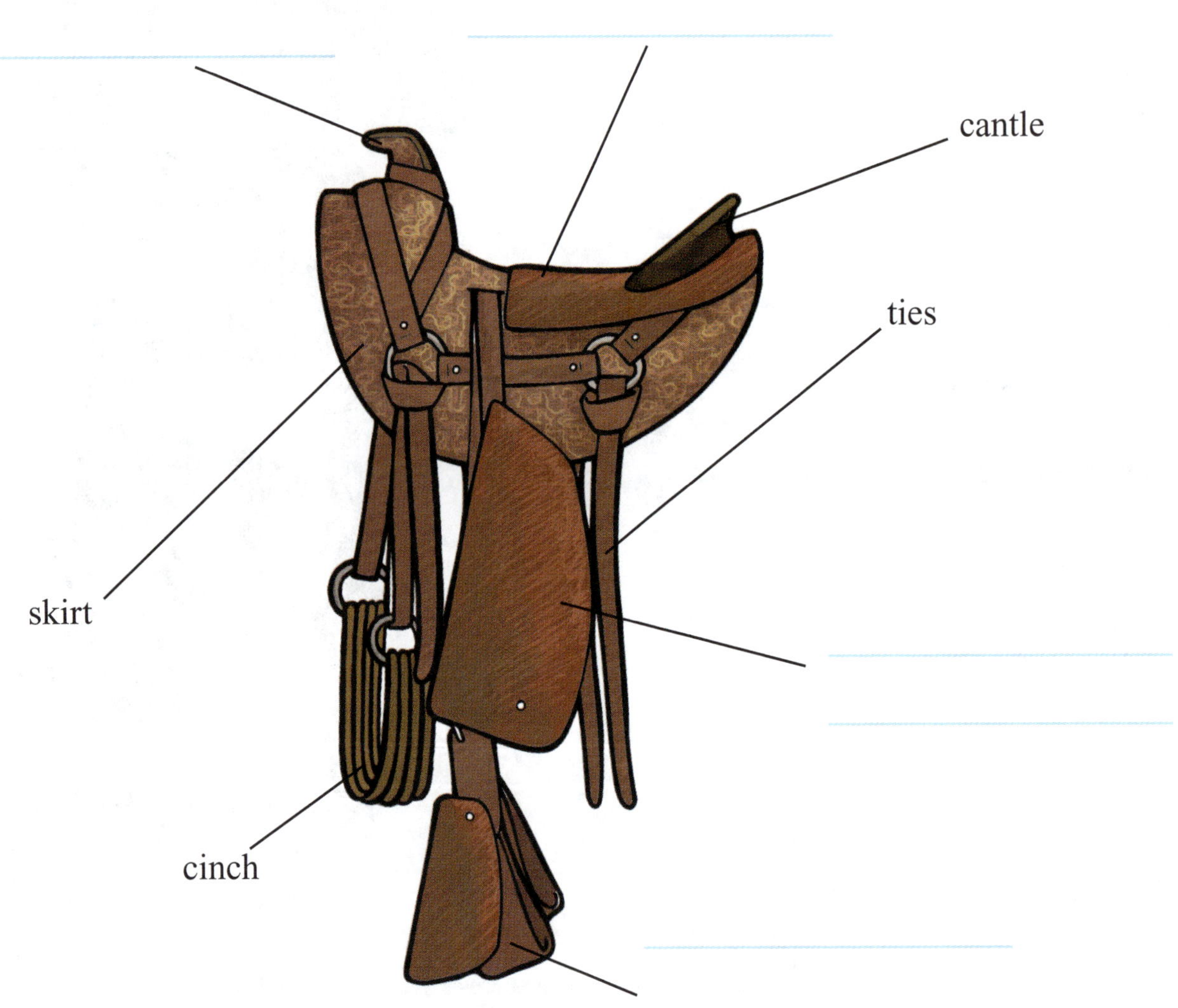

Name___________________________

1. Listen to the words as your teacher plays the recording.
   Sing the song together.

2. Underline phrases that are information you have read about in your text.

Chisholm Trail

Traditional

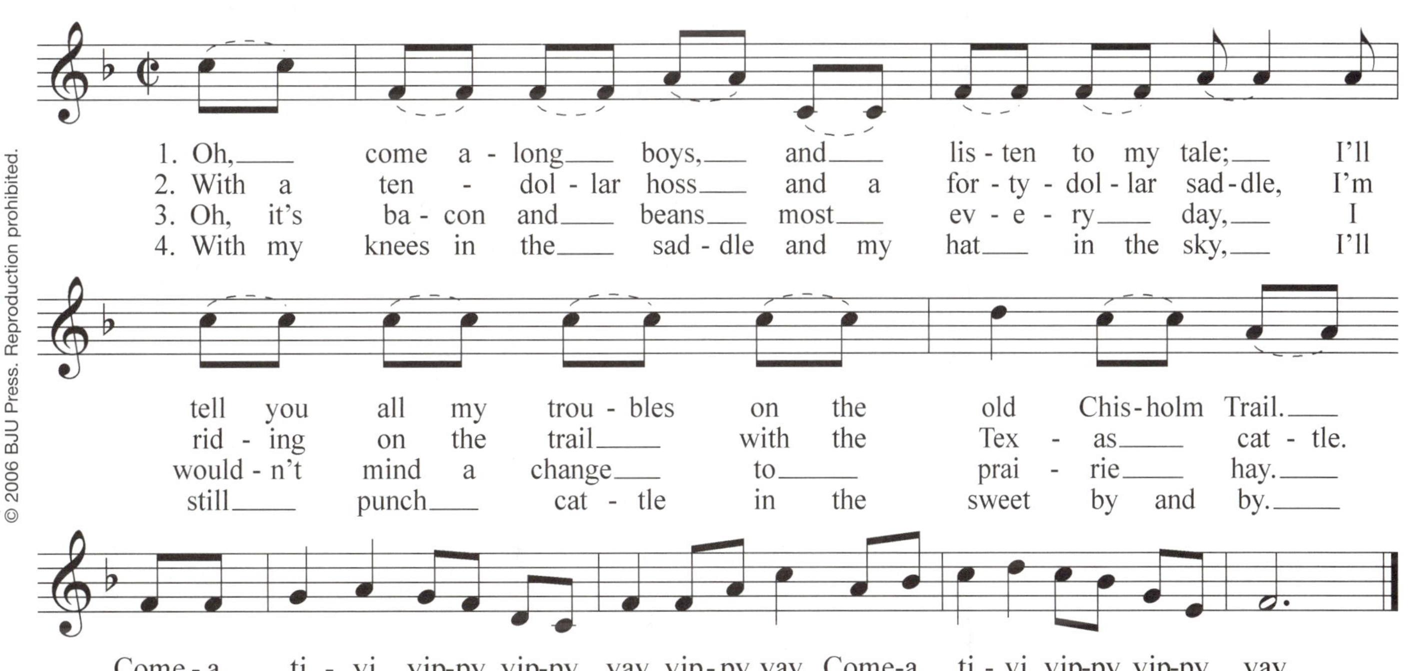

My Ranch

Name_______________________

Read the *Learning How* steps on text page 234.

1. Draw a star on the map where your ranch is located.

2. Draw a trail from your ranch to the nearest railroad.

3. Write the name of your ranch.

★ Ranch ________________________

4. Draw a picture of your ranch brand in the box.

Brand

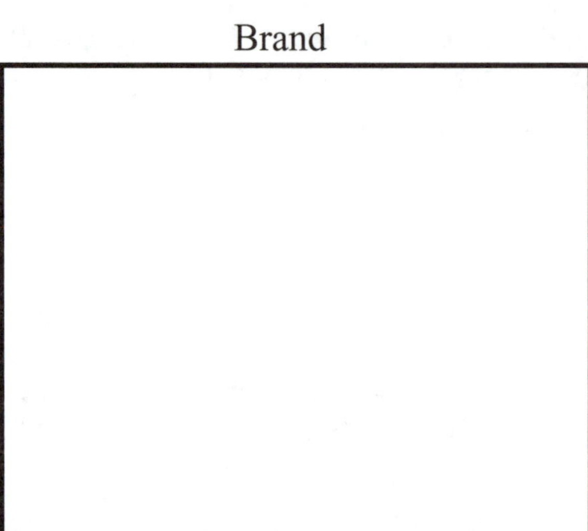

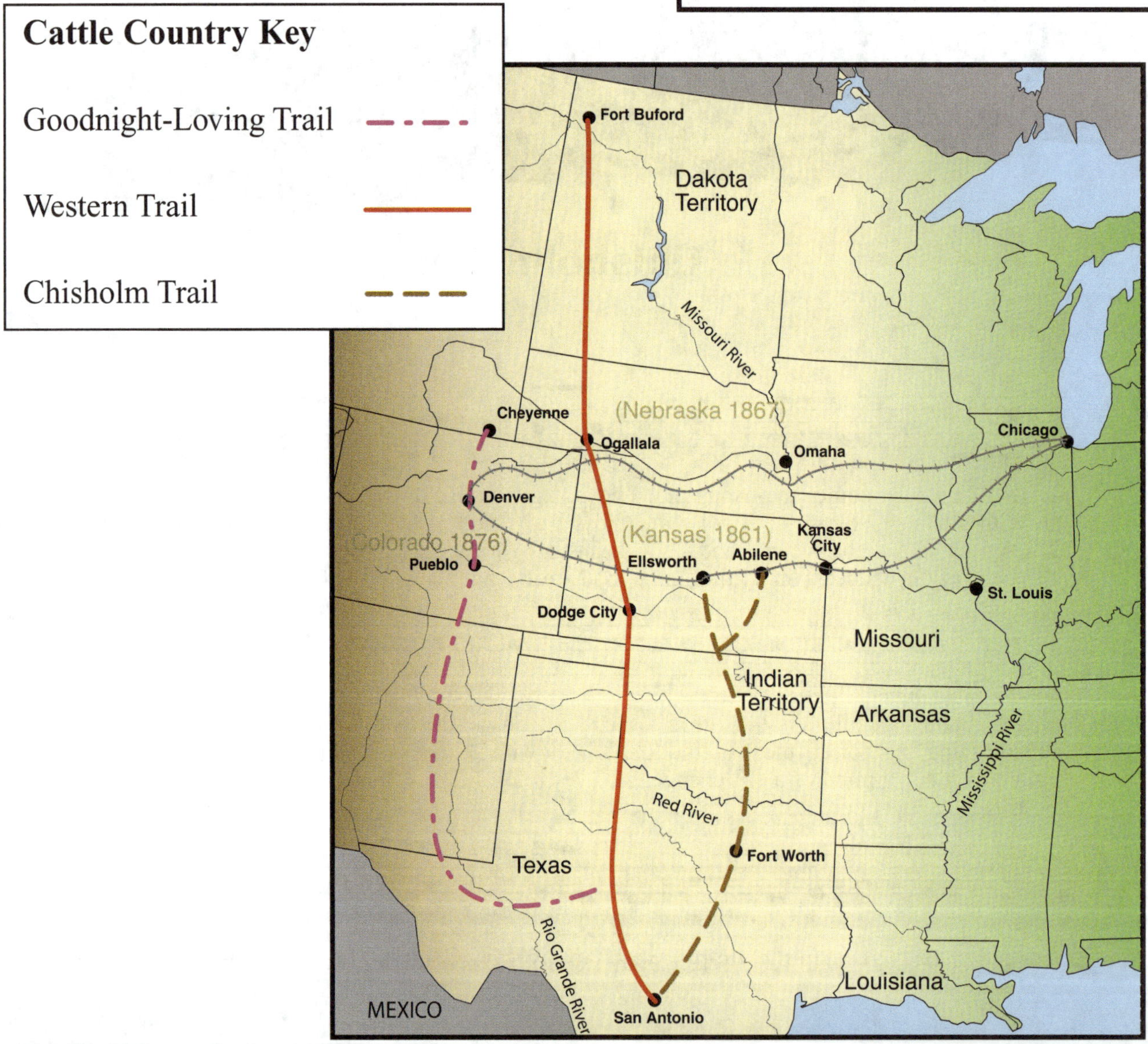

Name_______________________________

A. Draw a line to match the word to its definition.

1. cowboy

2. cattle drive

3. stampede

4. brand

A. to mark with a hot iron

B. a person who works with cattle

C. to run wild suddenly

D. moving of cattle from one place to another

B. Fill in the blanks using the word bank.

| branded | Homestead | rustlers | sod | thieves |

5. The West had some cattle ______________________ and many honest ranchers.

6. Settlers on the plains built their homes from ______________________ because there were not many trees.

7. The ______________________ Act promised settlers who lived on land for five years that they could own the land.

8. Cattle thieves were called ______________________.

9. Ranchers ______________________ their cattle so rustlers could not take them.

C. Write the ranching terms in the correct list.

| bandanna | branding iron | gauntlets | hat | lariat | saddle |

10. Cowboy's clothing: ______________________

11. Cowboy's equipment: ______________________

A cowboy's clothing served as his gear. His **hat** was used to carry water and fan a fire. A **bandanna** kept dust out of his nose and mouth and the sun off his neck. The large **gauntlets** the cowboy wore on his hands prevented rope burns and blisters.

Cavalry Hand Signals

Name________________________________

A. Follow your teacher's directions to sing this song.

To Horse

B. Read text pages 235–36 and the *Learning How* steps on text page 237. Write the letter of the picture on the blanks.

________ 1. Which picture shows Sergeant Madsen calling for attention?

________ 2. Which picture shows the riders are to form two lines?

________ 3. Which picture shows the riders are to go to the right?

A.

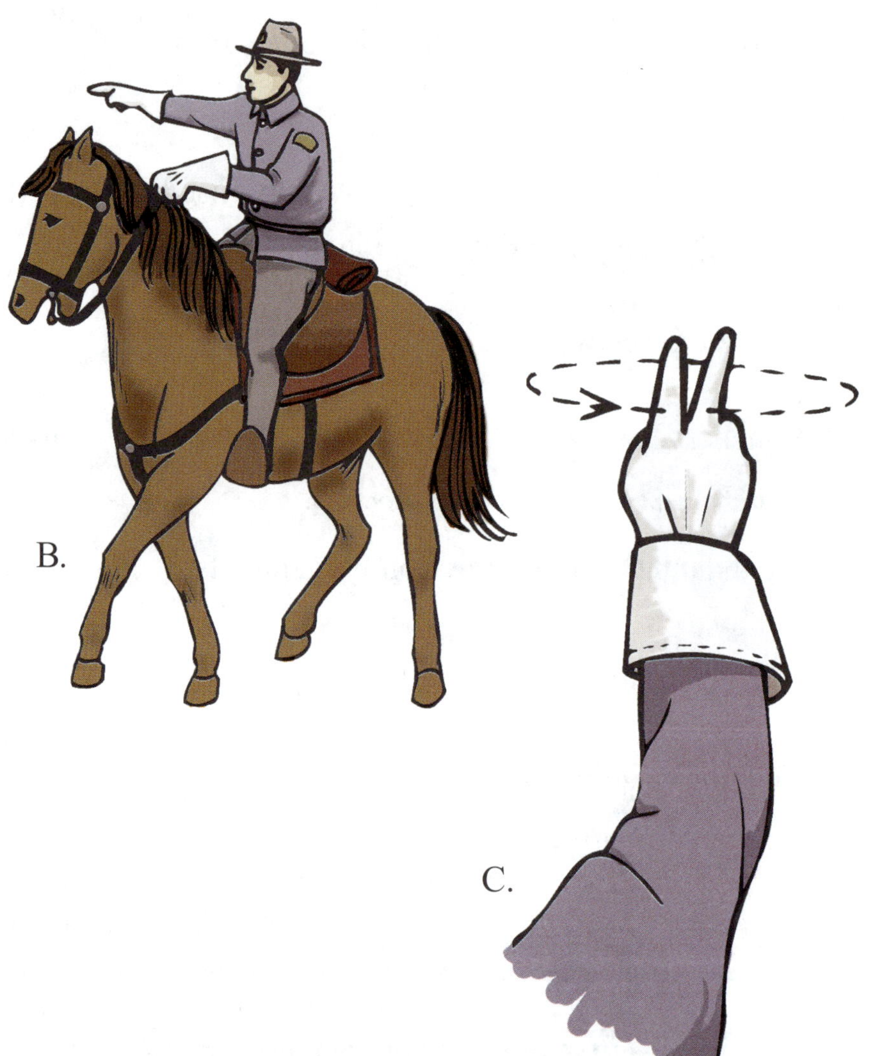

B.

C.

Cavalry Outpost

Name_______________________

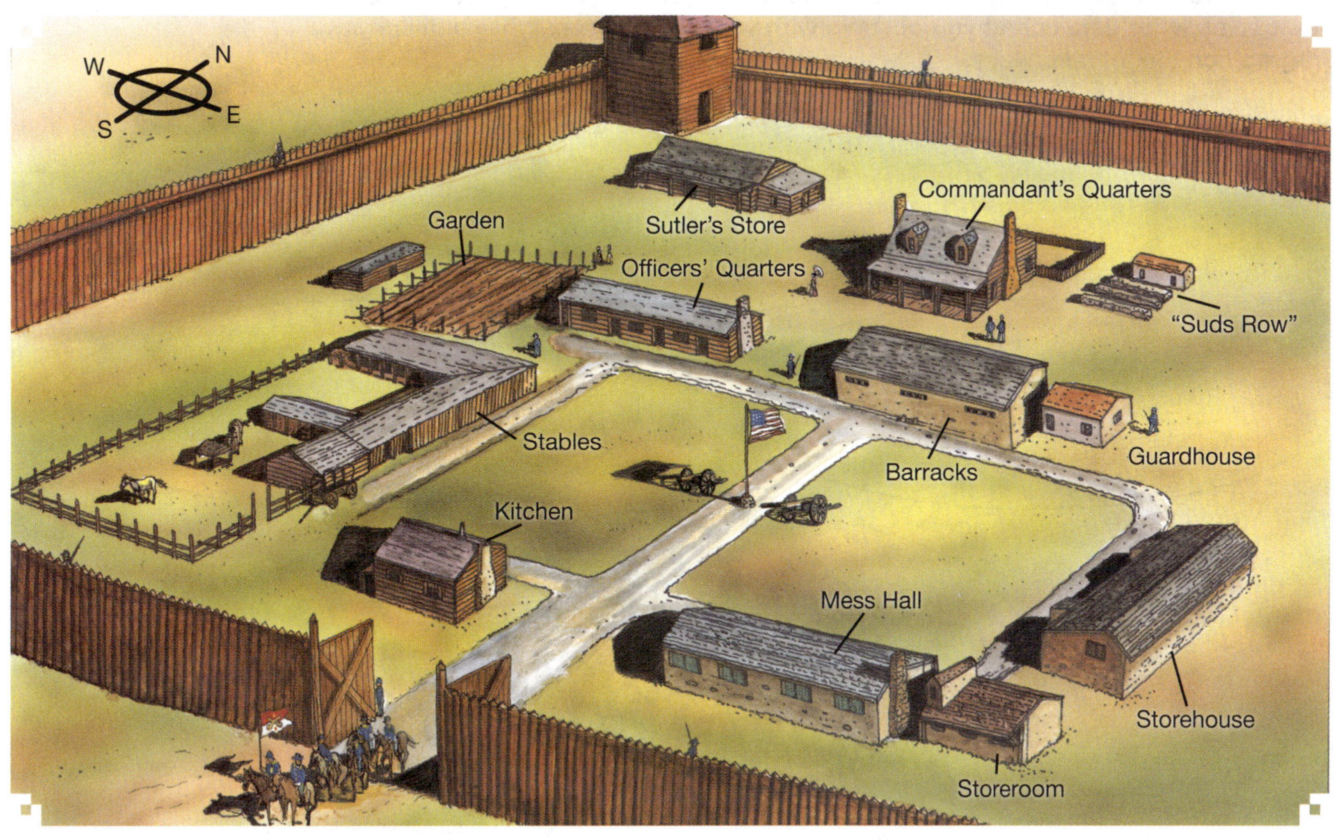

Use the map to fill in the circle.

1. What is closer to the center of the outpost?
   ○ "suds row"   ○ the American flag

2. Which is west of the kitchen?
   ○ the stables   ○ the mess hall

3. Which pair of buildings is farther apart?
   ○ the storeroom and the guardhouse   ○ the kitchen and Sutler's store

4. An officer must walk past the barracks to get from his quarters to _____.
   ○ the guardhouse   ○ the garden

5. What is between "suds row" and Sutler's store?
   ○ the commandant's quarters   ○ the barracks

6. Which is north of the officers' quarters?
   ○ the barracks   ○ Sutler's store

Cavalry Account

Name_______________________

Use the word web to help you see, hear, taste, smell, and feel cavalry life. In the outer circles write details that you observe with your five senses. Write a descriptive paragraph on life in the cavalry.

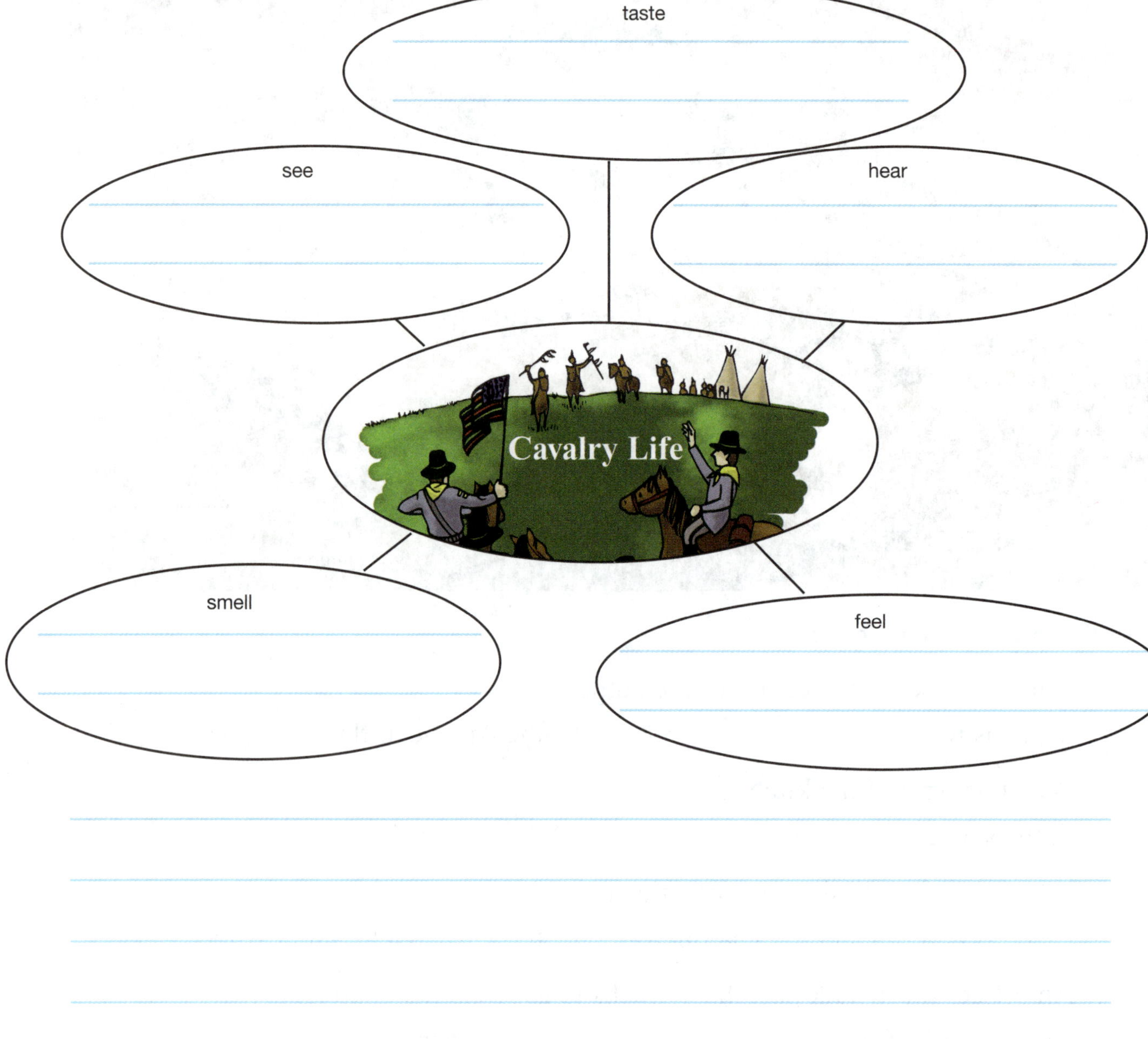

Heritage Studies 3
Worktext—Chapter 12

Name_______________________

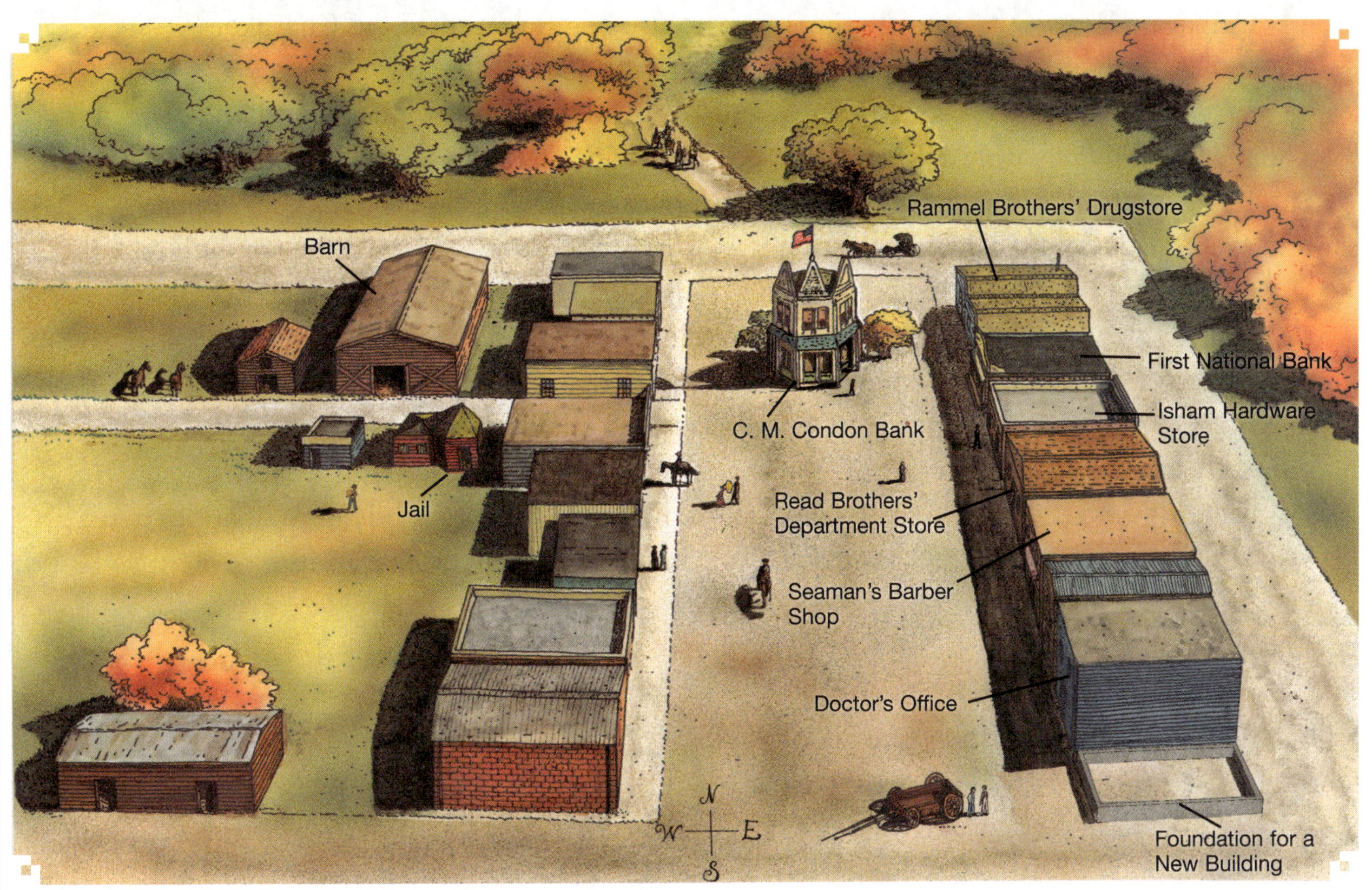

Use the map to fill in the circle.

1. When Marshal Connelly walks from the jail to Rammel Brothers' Drugstore, which direction does he travel?

   ○ east then north   ○ west then north

2. Which bank is farther east?

   ○ C. M. Condon Bank   ○ First National Bank

3. What is between the Isham Hardware Store and Rammel Brothers' Drugstore?

   ○ First National Bank   ○ the doctor's office

4. Who has to walk farther from the barn?

   ○ a cowboy going to get a haircut   ○ a cowboy going to C. M. Condon Bank

5. Which is south of Read Brothers' Department Store?

   ○ Rammel Brothers' Drugstore   ○ foundation for a new building

Cherokee Teacher

Name_______________________________

Catharine Brown was born in the forest of Alabama. Her Cherokee parents were Yau-nu-gung-yah-ski and Tsa-luh. Their English names were John and Sarah Brown. Catharine's father was an important leader in the Cherokee nation.

Catharine wanted to go to school. At seventeen, she was able to attend a mission school. There she learned in three months to read and write. Missionaries taught her how to read the Bible.

Catharine was excited to read that God was her Creator. She read that Jesus loved her and died for her. Soon she accepted Jesus as her Savior.

"I thank God, I am entirely in his hands," said Catharine. She wanted God to use her. She wanted the Cherokee people to know Jesus as Savior.

After leaving the mission school, Catharine started a school for the Cherokee people. She taught her people to read the Bible. They learned about God. The Cherokee people could read that Jesus died for them.

Catharine found ways to share Jesus' love. She invited her Cherokee friends for prayer and Bible reading. She went about doing good things for others. Catharine taught her people to love Jesus.

Catharine Brown learned to read the Bible at the Brainerd mission school.

Fill in the circle.

1. Catharine's father was an important leader of the ______.

   ○ Cherokee nation
   ○ Tsa-luh tribe

2. Catharine was ______.

   ○ seven years old when she learned to read
   ○ seventeen years old when she learned to read

3. Catharine opened ______.

   ○ a school to teach her people to read the Bible
   ○ an orphanage to care for Cherokee children

4. Catharine wanted the Cherokee people ______.

   ○ to be educated in American ways
   ○ to love Jesus

Heritage Studies 3
Worktext—Chapter 12

Name___________________________________

Sitting Bull would not give the **Black Hills** to the gold hunters. Many years earlier his people had been promised this land. The gold hunters did not follow the treaty. They ran the Plains people off the land. Sitting Bull and his people moved into the valley of the **Bighorn Mountains**. When Colonel Custer found them, he ordered an attack on the warriors. The battle took place near the Little Bighorn River. Custer and his men were killed in the Battle of Little Bighorn on **June 25, 1876**. This happened in what is present-day Montana.

1. Using the map key, draw small hills in the Black Hills area.

2. Using the map key, draw mountains in the Bighorn Mountains.

3. Put an *X* between Little Bighorn River and Rosebud Creek where the Battle of Little Bighorn took place. _______________________

4. What was the date of the Battle of Little Bighorn? _______________________

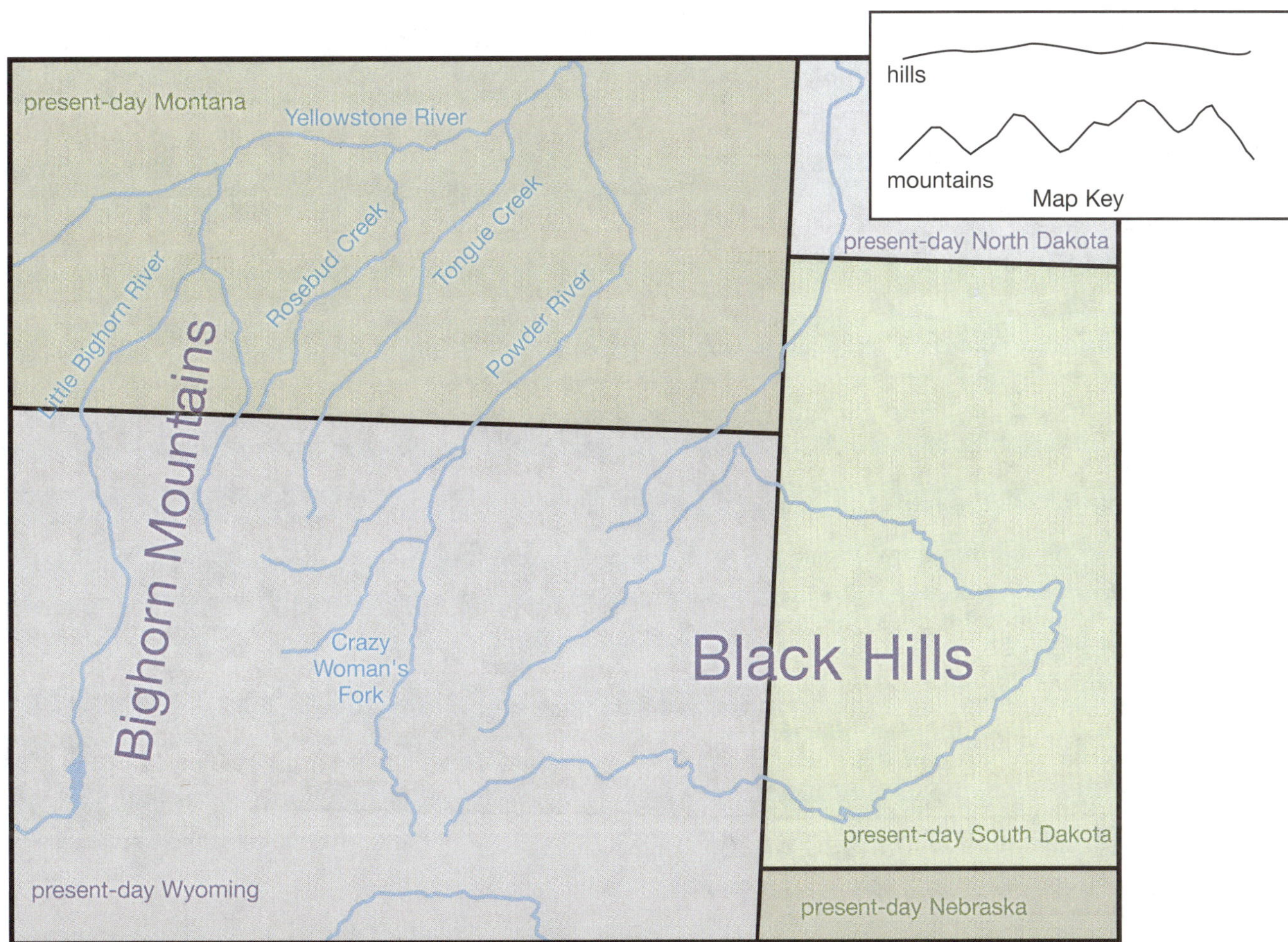

Sioux Reservations

Name_________________________________

Fill in the circle. You will need a ruler.

1. Since 1 inch represents 50 miles, 2 inches represents _____.

   ○ 100 miles   ○ 200 miles

2. The width of Rosebud Reservation is about _____.   ○ 50 miles   ○ 100 miles

3. To travel from Standing Rock Reservation to Pine Ridge Reservation, go _____.

   ○ east   ○ south

4. Fort Yates is on _____.   ○ Rosebud Reservation   ○ Standing Rock Reservation

5. Wounded Knee is on _____.

   ○ Pine Ridge Reservation   ○ Cheyenne River Reservation

6. The distance from Fort Meade to Fort Sully is _____.

   ○ about 150 miles   ○ about 300 miles

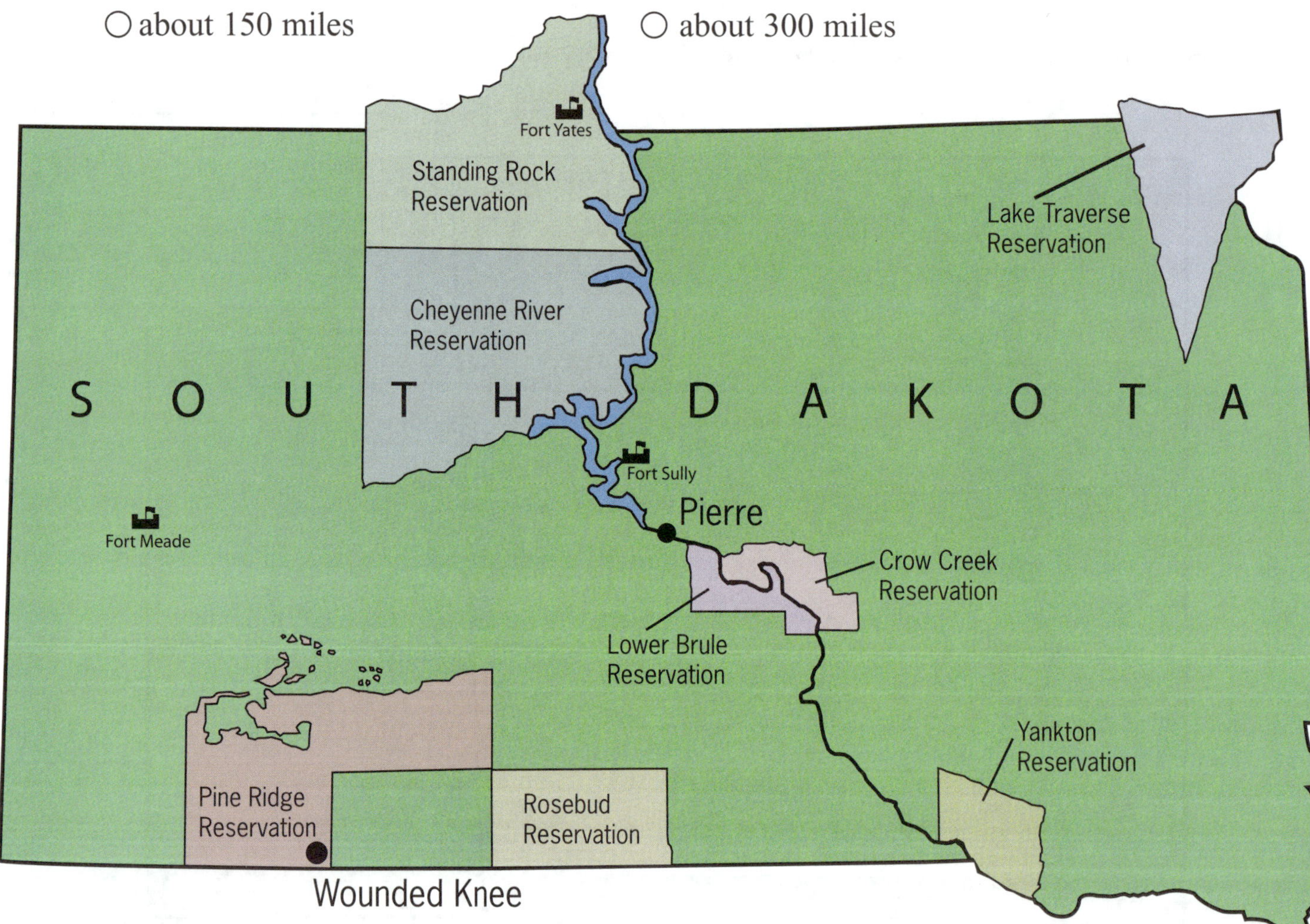

Heritage Studies 3
Worktext—Chapter 12

Name_______________________

Fill in the blanks using the word banks.

> brothers   bugle   cavalry

1. A cavalry horse recognized the _______________ tunes.

2. Soldiers rode horses in the _______________ part of the army.

3. The James _______________ robbed trains and banks.

> cavalry   Custer   settlers   treaty

4. The _______________ ran the Sioux off their land and broke the treaty with Spotted Tail.

5. These settlers were dishonest because they did not keep the _______________.

6. Some of the Sioux wanted to fight the _______________ because of the broken treaty.

7. Colonel _______________ led the cavalrymen to fight the Sioux.

> Bighorn   Custer   Sioux   Wounded

8. _______________ said, "I need no help." He was proud and impatient.

9. Custer lost all of his men at the Battle of Little _______________ in present-day Montana.

10. The warriors at _______________ Knee believed that if they wore "ghost shirts," no bullets could harm them.

11. The _______________ (or Plains Indians) never fought back again after the battle at Wounded Knee.

Name______________________________

A. Match the people with the description by writing the correct letter in the blanks.

______ 1. cowboys (230)   A. cattle thieves in the West

______ 2. cavalry (235)   B. Sioux, fought at Wounded Knee

______ 3. homesteaders (229)   C. work with cattle

______ 4. Plains Indians (242)   D. rode horses in the United States Army

______ 5. rustlers (232)   E. lived on land five years, became owners

**B. Match the descriptions with the people by writing the correct letter in the blanks.
(Some choices will be used more than once.)**

______ 6. broke treaty with Spotted Tail (240)

______ 7. branded cattle so rustlers could not take them (232)

______ 8. their horses recognized bugle tunes (235)

______ 9. believed "ghost shirts" would protect them from
bullets at Wounded Knee (242)

______ 10. made homes of sod; no trees to build houses (227–28)

______ 11. after Wounded Knee, never fought back again (242)

______ 12. proud and impatient colonel who lost the battle at
Little Bighorn in present-day Montana (241)

______ 13. two brothers who robbed trains and banks (239)

A. cavalry
B. ranchers
C. settlers
D. warriors
E. George Custer
F. Frank and Jesse
   James

C. Fill in the blanks about a cowboy using the word banks. (230–32)

| bandanna | gauntlets | hat | branding | drive | stampede |

14. A ________________ keeps dust out of the nose in a ________________.

15. A cowboy wears ________________ to protect his hands when

________________ cattle with a hot iron.

16. A cowboy needs to wear a ________________ while riding across the country

on a long cattle ________________.

PHOTO CREDITS

The following agencies and individuals have furnished materials to meet the photographic needs of this textbook. We wish to express our gratitude to them for their important contribution.

Abraham Lincoln Presidential Library & Museum
Architect of the Capitol
Art Resource
Cartesia Software
George Collins
COREL Corporation

iStock International Inc.
JUPITERIMAGES/Photos.com
Library of Congress
Mount Vernon Ladies' Association
National Archives
North Wind Picture Archives

PhotoDisc/Getty Images, Inc.
PhotosForMe
United States Air Force
United States House of Representatives
United States Marine Corps
Unusual Films

Front Cover
PhotoDisc/Getty Images, Inc. (eagle), © 2005 iStock International Inc. All rights reserved. (all others)

Front Matter
© 2005 iStock International Inc. (Mayflower), PhotoDisc/Getty Images, Inc. (Independence Hall), Library of Congress (Columbus, Washington), George Collins (Redcoats), Unusual Films (Constitution) vi

Chapter 1
Unusual Films 1–16 (bottom bar), 8 (background); Library of Congress 2, 4 (background, top left), 15 (background), 16 (background); Unusual Films 8 (background); Courtesy of the Mount Vernon Ladies' Association 14

Chapter 2
Réunion des Musées Nationaux/Art Resource, NY 18; © 2005 JUPITERIMAGES/Photos.com. All rights reserved. 20, 22 (background), 24 (background); United States Marine Corps 21

Chapter 3
Cartesia Software 25–34 (bottom bar), 27 (background), 29, 33–34 (background)

Chapter 4
Architect of the Capitol, Collection of the United States House of Representatives 38

Chapter 6
© 2005 iStock International Inc. All rights reserved. 63, 65, 67, 70 (top and middle), 71 (top both), 72; © 2005 JUPITERIMAGES/Photos.com. All rights reserved. 70 (bottom); COREL Corporation 71 (bottom)

Chapter 7
COREL Corporation 80, 86 (background); Library of Congress 81, 83 (bottom right), 84; Abraham Lincoln Presidential Library & Museum 83 (bottom left)

Chapter 8
Library of Congress 87; © 2005 iStock International Inc. All rights reserved. 90

Chapter 9
National Archives 95–102 (bottom bar), 96, 97, 101 (top right); North Wind Picture Archives 99 (bottom); Library of Congress 99 (background), 100 (all), 101 (left and both middle), 102 (background)

Chapter 10
PhotosForMe 103–10 (bottom bar), 105; United States Air Force 107 (background); © 2005 iStock International Inc. All rights reserved. 108

Chapter 11
COREL Corporation 111–22 (bottom bar), 112; Library of Congress 118